Saint Clare of Assisi

Volume One
The Original Writings

with an English tanslation notes by
Sr Frances Teresa Downing osc

Saint Clare of Assisi
Volume One, The Original Writings
Sr. Frances Teresa Downing osc

© 2012 Sr. Frances Teresa Downing osc
Book and cover design: Tau Publishing Design Dept.

Cover image of manuscript of St Clare's letters written ca. 1380 in St Agnes' monastery in Prague. Photo provided by Mons. Biagio Pizzi, library of the basilica of St Ambrogio, Milan, Italy.

For permission contact:
Tau Publishing, LLC
Permissions Dept.
4727 North 12th street
Phoenix, AZ 85014

ISBN: 978-1-61956-004-8

Published by Tau Publishing, LLC
www.Tau-Publishing.com
Printed in the United States of America.

Tau-publishing.com
Words of Inspiration

Sicut meridiana lux clara est

(Isaiah 18, 4)[1]

Table of Contents

Introduction

Some eight hundred years ago, Clare of Assisi left everything to join Francis and his companions in the same and common desire to journey in the footprints of Jesus Christ. They wanted to live according to the form of his holy Gospel. Radically, that is, following the poverty and the humility of Jesus. But, even though history attests that Clare, Francis, and his brothers were companions in the same evangelical endeavor, for too long a time, Clare has been kept in the shadow of Francis, relegated to merely a chapter of his life. Compared to the innumerable amount of studies on the *Poverello*, the Clarian bibliography is rather meager and repetitive. Fortunately, things have changed in recent times, and an increasing interest in Clare and the community of San Damiano has produced and continues to produce publications of high quality in various languages. The present book is timely, and definitely contributes a missing tool for those in the English-speaking audience who want to approach the Lady of Assisi.

Even though an English translation of some of Clare's writings had been published as part of or as an appendix to books released around the 700th anniversary of her death,[1] the English-speaking audience did not have access to a comprehensive translation of the writings of Clare until the early 1980s.[2] Moreover, a first critical edition of the writings of Clare – Latin text with French translation, introduction and notes – finally appeared in the mid-1980s.[3] That bilingual edition gave birth to versions in other languages like Italian, Portuguese and Polish.[4] The present edition is unique. Prepared by Sr. Frances Teresa Downing, it is the first comprehensive bilingual Latin-English edition of the writings of Clare, and it is also the first English translation of those writings by a woman, and a woman who is a sister of Clare's Order. This new translation follows closely the original Latin and, as such, is an intellectual work of quality. But it also proceeds from the heart and the love for Lady Clare, the Poor Sister of San Damiano in Assisi.

The renewed interest in Clare probably has several causes: one can be a current interest in women studies; another, an interest in medieval women in general, and in religious women of the Middle Ages in particular.[5] But the major generator of interest in Clare has probably been the rediscovery of the Franciscan movement, that is, of that first generation of men and women who followed Francis to form an evangelical *fraternitas* before it was progressively divided into separate canonical orders. That major religious movement of the 13th century is definitely drawing the interest of women and men, religious and lay folk, historians or not. And it has become progressively clearer that the study of Francis of Assisi and the Franciscan family cannot do without the historic and influential presence of Clare. She is unique as the first woman to join Francis and his brothers, opening the way for other women to develop a new way to live the Gospel. She will be the first woman to write a form of life – a rule – for women. After Francis' death in 1226, she will be the strong and faithful defender of his memory. And, until her death in 1253, she will remain for Francis' companions the point of reference, as she and San Damiano had been for Francis.

The writings of Clare that have found their way down to us are not many: a few letters, a testament, a blessing, and her form of life. Those writings are our first opportunity to reach Clare beyond the centuries of history between her and us today. They illustrate how outstanding a woman Clare was in her time, and how relevant she can still be today, for men and women, lay and religious alike. This is a woman who found her own way to be a true disciple of Jesus Christ. She knew who she was, she knew what she wanted. She was strong and compassionate. She was assertive and respectful. Her contemplation of Jesus was the source of her activity for the benefit of her community, of the Franciscan Order, of the Church and of her hometown.

She was peaceful, but she was also politically astute. She exemplified a truly Christian leadership: she was the sister-mother, the one who cares and provides what is needed, and also the one who is constantly working at building community through consensus. She was joyful and happy. But, above all and the source of it all, she was a passionate and fearless lover of the one she followed, the one whose poverty and humility she clung to, the one she embraced totally: Jesus Christ.

Thanks to her writings, Clare, the Lady of Assisi, the Poor Sister of San Damiano continues to shine.

Jean-François Godet-Calogeras

[1] Cf. Nesta de Robeck, St. Clare of Assisi, Milwaukee: The Bruce Publishing Company, 1951; Ignatius Brady – Sr. Mary Frances, The Legend and Writings of Saint Clare of Assisi, St. Bonaventure, N.Y.: The Franciscan Institute, 1953.

[2] Regis Armstrong – Ignatius Brady, Francis and Clare: The Complete Works, New York: Paulist Press, 1982.

[3] Marie-France Becker – Jean-François Godet – Thaddée Matura, Claire d'Assise: Écrits, Paris: Éditions du Cerf, 1985.

[4] Marie-France Becker – Jean-François Godet – Thaddée Matura – Giorgio Ginepro Zoppetti, Chiara d'Assisi: Scritti, Vicenza: Edizioni LIEF, 1986: José Carlos Corrêa Pedroso, Fontes Clarianas, Petrópolis: CEFEPAL, 1993, p. 167-214; Święci Franciszek i Klara z Asyżu: Pisma, wydanie lacińsko-polskie, Kraków-Warszawa: Wydawnictwo "M", 2002, p. 397-565.

[5] See, for instance, A History of Women in the West, Vol. II: Silences of the Middle Ages, Christiane Klapisch-Zuber, Editor, Cambridge-London: The Belknap Press of Harvard University Press, 1992.

Translator's Comments

It seems as if I have been tinkering with this translation ever since I can remember, and each time friends suggested I publish it, I panicked and said it was not ready. Finally, however, it has dawned on me that this process might continue indefinitely and that it is an imperfect world, bedevilled with imperfect translations. Here is another one!

I have tried to be faithful to the Latin, not only to the words but also to the inner meaning as far as I could discern it. While I hope it will be read by many more than my Poor Clare sisters, I also know the Poor Clares to be a particularly relevant audience whom I must not betray. I have been aware, too, that in many Poor Clare houses the Form of Life and the Testament are read aloud regularly, so the text needed to read as English which would fall easily on the ear. This was particularly challenging given Clare's long Latin sentences, with their innumerable sub-clauses and parentheses which do not go easily into neat English sentences. I have finally come to recognise that, in spite of all its imperfections, this translation is probably as good as I can make it.

I would like especially to express my appreciation of the courtesy of Jeff Campbell and his team at Tau Publishers in agreeing to English spelling. This is why people of the United States will find such things as *honour* instead of *honor*, and *sympathise* for *sympathize*, *fulfil* for *fulfill* and many more. We also use commas slightly differently and far fewer semi-colons, but I hope very much that these details will not inhibit anyone from getting in touch with the message and guidance of Saint Clare, which are still so relevant for us today.

With my prayers
Sr Frances Teresa Downing osc
3 May 2011

Acknowledgements

It is certainly true that we stand on the backs of giants. I have been the beneficiary of so much critical and scholarly work, especially that done on the Continent, and hope here to make some of that scholarship available to an English-speaking audience. For each text, I have used the most recent critical edition, always with an eye on the work of earlier scholars.

For the **Rule** I have used the edition of 2003 produced by the Poor Clares of Italy working with Don Felice Accrocca. For the **Letters** I have made use of the scholarship of Fr Pozzi and Dr Beatrice Rima. This 1999 text is the most recent and is particularly interesting since it studies the letters as poetry and, as will be evident, raises interesting questions by making no concessions to ecclesiastical Latin. The numerous references to **Celano** in the section on the letters is the work of Fr Giovanni Boccali ofm. The echoes between Clare and Celano are a largely unexplored ground, though any forays into this territory have proved rich and rewarding. Anybody wanting further references to other early Franciscan texts cannot do better than consult *Opuscula S. Francisci et Scripta S. Clarae Assisiensium* edited and annotated by Giovanni Boccali ofm.[2] There, after each text, is a large *apparatus criticus* which it is quite impossible to reproduce here but which repays any effort to explore.

The letter to **Ermentrude** raises some issues which I have summarised briefly in the introduction, as does the **Testament** and its authenticity. For both those texts and for the **Blessing** of Clare, I have used that given in the French *Ecrits* of 1985. All these are used with the generous permission of the copyright holders, for which I am very grateful.

Scripture references (in English) are given as footnotes on the Latin side of the book, while other references, mainly to Franciscan sources, are on the right. In the Rule, any comments or explanatory notes are printed as end notes at the close of each chapter. This can be irritating for the reader, but proved unavoidable because had they all been footnotes, there would have been little room for the text itself.

On the nuts and bolts level, I owe a big debt of gratitude to many who have generously made available their skills and time, but I must especially mention Graham Wheater who read everything and missed nothing and any typos which remain have certainly crept in later.

2   Ed. Porziuncola 1978

I also want to pay even greater tribute to Mary Esther Stewart who also read everything and missed nothing, who coped with preparing this complicated text for the printers and watched over its journey through the press. I am very appreciative of her expertise, patience and co-operation as of that which we have received from Jeff Campbell at Tau Publishing. I wish, too, to mention those Poor Clare sisters who have read various versions and shared their thoughts and comments with me, always helpfully. I also owe a debt to those I have worked with in various meetings and workshops as well as at the Franciscan International Study Centre, Canterbury. Using the text in this way has been such a help in teasing out the meaning and putting it into the words of today.

I sincerely thank Dr Jean-François Godet-Calogeras, both for his Introduction, his sharp eye for typing or translating errors, and for the encouragement he gave me so consistently and generously and which I have so much valued. I also want to thank Fr Murray Bodo ofm for reading through the translation of the letters with me, so that they sounded as much as possible like 'English English' and not like a translation, and for the great help he gave me in understanding the inner poetry of Clare's words.

Finally, I must thank both Murray Bodo and André Cirino ofm for their insistence that I make a start on this work, keep at it and bring it to a conclusion, as well as for their unfailing support, encouragement and affirmation. A particular debt is owed to André Cirino; this project (among others) was his brainchild and without his energy and commitment and, on occasion his brotherly pushing, I know I would have gone on indefinitely tinkering with the translation and finalising nothing. I would like him to be happy with the result.

General Sources

Chiara d'Assisi: Lettere ad Agnese La visione dello specchio, Giovanni Pozzi e Beatrice Rima, Adelphi Edizioni, Milan 1999.

Chiara di Assisi e le Sue Fonti Legislative, Federazione S. Chiara di Assisi delle Clarisse di Umbria-Sardegna, Sinossi Cromatica, Volume 1, Edizioni Messaggero Padova, Padua 2003.

Claire d'Assise, Ecrits, Marie-France Becker, Jean-François Godet, Thaddée Matura, Les Editions du Cerf, Paris 1985.

Clare of Assisi: The Lady, Early Documents, Edited and translated by Regis Armstrong, 2nd edition, New City Press, New York, 2006

Francis' Rule for Hermitages: Dissertationes ad Lauream by Artemio Raymundo omf cap, Pontificium Athenaeum Antonianum, Rome 1994.

Opuscula S. Francisci et Scripta S. Clarae Assisiensium, cura e studio Ioannis M. Boccali, Italian translation by Luciano Canonici, Edizioni Porziuncola, Assisi 1978.

Background References for the Form of Life

Chapter 2 - *The* S*triped Mantle of the Poor Clares: Image and Text in Italy in the Later Middle Ages* by Cordelia Warr, in *Arte Cristiana* 86 (1998): 415-430.

Chapter 3 - *The Origins of the Modern Roman Liturgy* by Peter van Dijk and Joan H Walker, Newman Press, Darton, Longman and Todd, London 1960)

Chapter 4 - *Saepe enim Dominus quod melius est minori revelat: A five-hundred year-old erroneous reading* by Sr Chiara Agnese Acquadro osc, Greyfriars Review 17 (2003).

Background References for the Testament

Chiara d'Assisi, La questione dell'autenticità del Privilegium Paupertatis e del Testamento by Werner Maleczek, translated by M. P. Alberzoni, Edizioni Biblioteca Francescana, Milan 1996.

Abbreviation

Letters of Saint Francis:

LtLeo	Letter to Brother Leo
LtR	Letter to the Rulers of the People
1LtCl	First Letter to All Clerics
2LtCl	Second Letter to All Clerics
1LtF	First Letter to the Faithful
2LtF	Second Letter to the Faithful
LtMin	Letter to a Minister
1LtCus	First Letter to the Custodians
2LtCus	Second Letter to the Custodians
LtAnt	Letter to Brother Anthony
LtOrd	Letter to the Whole Order
LtElias	A Letter to Brother Elias
	(not accepted as authentic by all scholars)

Other Writings of Saint Francis

Adm	Admonitions
1Reg	Earlier Rule of 1221
2Reg	Later Rule of 1223
1TestF	Testament
2TestF	Testament of Siena
Cant	Canticle of the Creatures
AudPov	*Audite poverelle* - Canticle of Exhortation to St Clare and Her Sisters
RegEr	Rule for Hermitages
PrOF	Prayer Inspired by the Our Father
SalV	Salutation of the Virtues
BLeo	Blessing for Brother Leo
UltVol	Last Will of Francis for St Clare and Her Sisters

Writings of Saint Clare

TestCl	Testament of Clare
BlCl	Blessing of Clare
RegCl	Rule of Clare
1LtAg	First Letter of Clare to Agnes of Prague
2LtAg	Second Letter of Clare to Agnes of Prague
3LtAg	Third Letter of Clare to Agnes of Prague
4LtAg	Fourth Letter of Clare to Agnes of Prague
LtErm	Letter to Ermintrude

Early Sources

ProcCan	Process of Canonisation for Saint Clare
BullCan	Bull of Canonisation for Saint Clare
RegInn	Rule of Innocent IV
RegHug	Rule of Hugolino (Gregory IX)
1Cel	First Life of Francis by Thomas of Celano
2Cel	Second Life of Francis by Thomas of Celano
L3C	Legend of the Three Companions
RegSB	Rule of St Benedict

Other Sources

AFH	*Archivum Franciscanum Historicum*
BF	*Bullarium Franciscanum*

General Introduction to the Letters of Saint Clare

Mediaeval letter writing was known as the *ars dictandi*, the art of dictating. In an age in which literacy was rare, this tells us that it was normal to have a secretary who wrote at dictation. This tended to impose strict norms to which the writer (speaker) had to conform. Social rank governed everything including style in letter writing.

The subdivisions of a properly written letter were each governed by rigid principles and this even included the grammar and the case in which greetings and good wishes could be couched. A letter always opened with an announcement concerning both the recipient and the writer, the one higher in social rank coming first. Good wishes must be exchanged but certain wishes must be avoided or disguised with adjectives. It was good to wish *salutem et pacem* – salvation or health which was considered to be connected, and peace, but *salutem* on its own was considered blunt and crude. The purpose was to make the recipient receptive of what was to come in the letter, not to cast doubts on their salvation. Such bluntness needed to be softened with catch-all phrases such a *quidquid* or *quod: salute et quidquid desiderari potestyt* or as Clare said to Agnes (1.2) *recommendationem sui omnimodam.*

In the main part of the letter, the *narratio,* it was normal to start with encouragement (1.3) before going on to the substance of the letter. Points of transition were marked with certain bridging words: *hinc est* (1.5), *ergo* (1.12), *si ergo* (1.19), *enim* (1.25), *quippe* (1.30), *cum vero* (2.8), *sed quia* (2.10), *in hoc autem* (2.15).

It was correct to sprinkle the letter with titles *regina* (2. 20) *domina* (2, 24; 3, 11) and descriptive words, as Clare uses *carissima* (3, 10 & 40); *soror* (1, 12) *filia* (4. 39). She rarely speaks in the first person with the major exception of the word *gaudere,* or *exultare.* She uses the first 19 times across the four letters.

Titles are used to refer to nobility and rank. Agnes' nobility is underlined, she is related to the King as daughter and later sister but in 2Ag and 4Ag a different genealogy is referred to where she is Queen because of Christ. Clare never uses the titles of religious life, never names herself or Agnes as Abbess but only sister among *cunctis mortalibus,* among all those destined for death. She uses *soror* but as a New Testament term, not a title of religious life, preferring *famula* and *serva* to all others.

For the institution, she defines the community as *pauper* or *incluse, dominarum inclusarum, pauperem dominarum. Pauperes* and *inclusae* have a juridical value. Gregory tended to use *reclusae* (closer to solitary) for 'his' group. Clare speaks of the monastery but not of the Order, just as she never uses *monache* or nuns.

Given the background and the tensions with Gregory's *Ordo Sancti Damiani* it is probable that every word was loaded and conveyed information to Agnes by subtle manipulation of nuances in a way which is not easy for us to grasp today.

This all shows us that Clare's letters were carefully constructed works of literature, skilful communications in which respect for the recipient was honoured by the beauty of the language. It is more than likely that she too had a secretary just as Francis did, which is why the art of writing letters was called the art of dictating. It is equally possible that the beauty of the Latin and the subtlety of the expression owe something (at least) to the skills of this unknown secretary. On the other hand, it should also be borne in mind that Clare was a well-educated woman from a social class steeped in the culture of the time. The most notable aspect of her letters is the consistency of the spirituality and the language, which strongly suggests that essentially these were her own composition.

The letters of Clare to Agnes of Prague also stand as a testament to a wonderful friendship. We see this friendship deepen and develop as we read through the text, and by the time we reach the fourth letter, we touch and are ourselves warmed by the intensity of love which that letter conveys. They not only touch us for what they reveal but they also stir us with a desire both to be loved like that by Clare and also to be able ourselves to know such intense feeling and commitment to another.

The First Letter
of Saint Clare to
Saint Agnes of Prague

1234–1238

The First Letter of Saint Clare to Saint Agnes

Context and Date

This letter is generally dated between 1234 and 1238,[a] mainly because it seems to be addressed to someone at the beginning of a committed life, which was Agnes' situation at this time. The language is formal, courteous and addressed to one who is socially superior. Clare addresses Agnes as the daughter of the King of Bohemia, her secular title, although it is possible that she had already entered the convent which she had built in Prague. The letter is clearly written after Agnes' refusal to marry the Emperor Frederick II, at which time she had also announced her desire to enter religious life and had appealed to Gregory IX for support in this. As was often the case, Gregory's support was motivated by his need for the political support of the King, first Agnes' father and later her loved brother Wenceslaus. There is not enough internal evidence to date the letter any more definitely than this. It may not have been Clare's first letter to Agnes since we know that Clare sent her four gifts on her entry into religion,[b] and this letter does not seem to be a covering letter for gifts. As so often with Clare, we only have some bits of the jigsaw.

Theme

The theme of the letter is spelt out in verse 6, where Clare speaks of the exchange which Agnes has made in choosing holy poverty and physical hardship instead of the privileges of being empress. Clare then goes on to speak of that other archetypal exchange made by the Son of God in His option for most high poverty, and how He did this in order to do battle with the enemy. In a passage replete with mediaeval symbolism, Clare describes how Agnes has also enrolled in this warfare, marching with Christ under the banner of poverty and virginity. She also links Agnes' choice with that of her patron, St Agnes the Roman martyr and does this by quoting from the liturgy for St Agnes feast on 21 January where St Ambrose in his turn quotes from the (then well-known) *Legend* of Agnes.

Things to note

Note especially the recurrence of groups of three, three adjectives, three nouns, three thoughts. This would say more powerfully to the mediaeval mind than to us that the letter focuses around the Trinity. It deals with Agnes' option for God, always within the context of God's option for us.

Note the comparisons with Agnes the Roman Martyr. We should bear in mind that she was a primary model for women at that time.

Note the paradox of surrender leading to virginity, poverty leading to infinite riches, and how Clare develops these themes, skilfully weaving them together.

Note also the mediaeval rather phonetic spelling which is that used in the oldest existing manuscript of Clare's letters from which this text is taken. See **Notes** for more detailed comments about Clare's letters.

[1] Venerabili et sanctissime virgini domine Agneti, filie excellentissimi ac illustrissimi regis Bohemie, [2] Clara indigna famula Ihesu Christi et ancilla inutilis[1] dominarum inclusarum monasterii Sancti Damiani de Assisio, sua ubique subdita et ancilla, recommendacionem sui omnimodam cum reverencia speciali et eterne felicitatis gloriam adipisci.[2]

[3] Vestre sancte conversacionis et vite honestissime famam audiens, que non solum michi sed fere in toto est orbe terrarum[3] egregie divulgata, gaudeo plurimum in Domino et exulto, [4] de quo non tantum ego singularis valeo exsultare, sed universi qui faciunt et facere desiderant servitium Ihesu Christi.

[5] Hinc est quod, cum perfrui potuissetis pre ceteris pompis et honoribus et seculi dignitate, cum gloria excellenti valentes inclito cesari legitime desponsari, sicut vestre ac eius excellencie decuisset, [6] que omnia respuentes, toto animo et cordis affectu magis sanctissimam paupertatem et corporis penuriam elegistis, [7] sponsum nobilioris generis accipientes Dominum Ihesum Christum, qui vestram virginitatem semper immaculatam custodiet et illesam.

---

1   Cf. Lk 17, 10; cf.. Sir 50, 5.
2   Sir 50, 5.
3   Cf. 1 Thess 1, 8; Hab 3, 18.

[1] To the honoured and most holy virgin, the Lady Agnes, daughter of the Most Excellent and Most Illustrious King of Bohemia;[c] [2] Clare the unworthy family servant of Jesus Christ, and the unprofitable handmaid of the cloistered ladies[d] of the monastery of San Damiano, everywhere subject to her [the Lady Agnes] and her handmaid, recommends herself in every way with particular respect that she may come to the glory of eternal happiness.

[3] I rejoice often in the Lord, and I exult on hearing the unquestionable fame of Your[e] holy conduct and life. It is common knowledge, not only to me but to almost all the world. [4] Because of this it is not only I who am rejoicing but everyone who works or wants to work in the service of Jesus Christ.

[5] In fact You, more than most, could have thoroughly enjoyed the pomps, honours and grandeur of the world. You could quite legitimately have been married to the illustrious Caesar[f] and with outstanding glory, as would have been fitting to both Your and His Excellence. [6] Instead You have rejected all that. With Your whole being and Your whole heart, You have chosen most holy poverty and physical hardship. [7] You have taken to Yourself a far more noble kind of bridegroom, the Lord

[8] *Quem cum amaveritis casta estis, cum tetigeritis mundior* efficiemini, *cum acceperitis virgo estis,* [9] *cuius possibilitas forcior, generositas celsior, cuius aspectus pulchrior, amor suavior et omnis gracia elegancior,* [10] cuius *estis iam amplexibus astricta, qui pectus vestrum ornavit lapidibus preciosis, et vestris auribus tradidit inestimabiles margaritas,* [11] *et* totam *circumdedit vernantibus atque choruscantibus gemmis,* atque vos coronavit *aurea corona signo sanctitatis expressa.*[4]

[12] Ergo, soror carissima ymmo domina nimium veneranda, quia sponsa et mater estis et soror domini mei Ihesu Christi,[5] [13] virginitatis inviolabilis et paupertatis sanctissime vexillo resplendentissime insignita, in sancto servicio confortamini pauperis crucifixi, ardenti desiderio inchoato, [14] qui pro nobis omnibus *crucis sustinuit* passionem,[6] *eruens nos de potestate* principis *tenebrarum,*[7] qua ob transgressionem primi parentis vincti vinculis tenebamur, et *nos reconcilians*[8] Deo Patri.

---

4   Sir 45, 14.
5   Mt 12, 50.
6   Heb 12, 2.
7   Col 1, 13.
8   2 Cor 5, 18.

Jesus Christ, who will keep Your virginity unmarked and unimpaired forever.

[8] *Loving Him, You are chaste; touching Him, You are made pure; taking Him to Yourself, You are a virgin.* [9] *His resources are stronger, His generosity more heavenly, His appearance more beautiful, His love sweeter, and His every grace more attractive.* [10] *Now you are held in the close embrace of the One who has adorned Your breast with precious stones, and offered [You] priceless pearls for your ears,* [11] *and has completely surrounded You with spring-like and shining jewels, and He has crowned You with a coronet of gold, the particular sign of holiness.*[9]

[12] Therefore, my dearest sister or – as I should say Lady greatly respected, for You are the spouse, the mother and the sister of my Lord, Jesus Christ[10] – [13] You are so splendidly distinguished by the banner of inviolable virginity and most holy poverty. So be strengthened in the holy service of the poor Crucified One, begun with burning desire. [14] He took up the cross of His passion for the sake of us all, snatching us from the power of the prince of darkness in whose bondage we were held bound by the sin of our first parents, reconciling us with God the Father.

---

9   From the Breviary, January 21. The Passion of St Agnes the Roman Martyr.

10   2LetF 49-50.

[15] O beata paupertas, que diligentibus et amplexantibus eam divitias prestat eternas.

[16] O sancta paupertas, quam habentibus et desiderantibus a Deo celorum regnum promittitur et eterna gloria vitaque beata procul dubio exhibetur.[11]

[17] O pia paupertas, quam Dominus Ihesus Christus, qui celum terramque regebat et regit, qui dixit etiam et sunt facta, dignatus est pre ceteris amplexari.[12]

---

11   Cf. Mt 5, 3.
12   Ps 32, 9; Ps 148, 5.

[15] O blessed poverty,
who guarantees eternal riches
to those who love and embrace her.

[16] O holy poverty,
to those who hold her and long for her,
God has promised the Kingdom of heaven
and without any doubt
she shows us eternal glory and the blessed life.

[17] O faithful poverty,
the Lord Jesus Christ,
who ruled and still rules heaven and earth
since He spoke and they were made,
held you to be worth embracing before all else.

[18] *Vulpes* enim *foveas* inquit *habent et volucres celi nidos, filius autem hominis,* id est Christus, *non habet ubi caput reclinet*[13] sed *inclinato capite tradidit spiritum.*[14]

[19] Si ergo tantus et talis dominus in uterum veniens virginalem, despectus, egenus et pauper in mundo voluit apparere,[15] [20] ut homines, qui erant pauperrimi et egeni, celestis pabuli sufferentes nimiam egestatem, efficerentur in illo divites, regna celestia possidendo,

[21] exultate plurimum et gaudete, replete ingenti gaudio et leticia spiritali,[16] [22] quia cum vobis magis placuisset contemptus seculi quam honores, paupertas quam divitie temporales, et magis thesauros in celo recondere quam in terra, [23] *ubi nec* rubigo consumit *nec tinea demolitur et fures non effodiunt nec furantur,*[17] *merces vestra copiosissima est in celis*[18] [24] et fore digne meruistis soror, sponsa et mater altissimi Patris filii et gloriose virginis nuncupari.

---

13   Mt 8, 20; Lk 9, 58.

14   Jn 19, 30.

15   Cf. 2 Cor 8, 9.

16   Cf. Hab 3, 18.

17   Mt 6, 20.

18   Mt 5, 12.

[18] The foxes have holes, He said, and the birds of the air have nests. The Son of Man, that is Christ, has nowhere to lay His head but bowing His head, He gave up the Spirit.

[19] So if, on coming to the virginal womb, such a Lord (and so great a Lord) wanted to be seen in the world as a despised, needy and poor man, [20] it was so that the most poor and needy who were starving to death for lack of this heavenly food, might be enriched in Him by possessing the Kingdom of Heaven.

[21] Exult all the more and rejoice, be filled with tremendous joy and spiritual happiness! [22] For You, who were more pleased by the world's scorn than by its honours, by poverty than by temporal riches, You have hidden your treasure in heaven rather than on earth. [23] There neither rust consumes nor moth devours and thieves neither break in nor steal. In heaven Your reward overflows most abundantly. [24] Also You have, quite rightly, merited to be named the sister, spouse and mother of the Son of the Most High Father and the glorious Virgin.

[25] Credo enim firmiter vos novisse, eo quod regnum celorum nonnisi pauperibus a Domino promittitur et donatur, quia dum res diligitur temporalis, fructus amittitur caritatis, [26] *Deo et mammone deservire non posse*, quoniam *aut unus diligitur et alter odio habetur* et *aut uni* serviet *et alterum contempnet*,[19] [27] et vestitum cum nudo certare non posse, quia cicius ad terram deicitur qui habet unde teneatur, [28] et gloriosum manere in secolo et illic regnare cum Christo. Et quoniam *foramen acus* poterit *transire camelus* scandere *quam dives celica regna*[20]

[29] ideo abiecistis vestimenta, videlicet divicias temporales, ne luctanti succumbere penitus valeretis, ut per arctam viam et angustam portam possitis regna celestia introire.[21]

---

19   Mt 6, 24.
20   Mt 19, 24.
21   Cf. Mt 7, 13-14.

[25] For I firmly believe You to have understood that the Kingdom of Heaven is given and promised by the Lord only to the poor, for while someone is loving temporal things, they are losing the fruit of charity. [26] God and mammon cannot both be served, for either one will be loved and the other hated, or one will be served and the other despised. [27] Someone who is clothed cannot fight someone who is stripped naked, because the one who offers more to be held on to is more quickly thrown to the ground.[22] [28] And we cannot be in glory in this world and reign in the other with Christ. A camel will be able to go through the eye of a needle before a rich man can clamber up into heaven.

[29] This is why having thrown aside Your clothes (that is Your temporal riches) lest You surrender to the one who wrestles with You, You can therefore enter the heavenly Kingdom by the straight road and the narrow gate.

---

22   Cf. Homily of St Gregory *In evangelium XXXII.*

[30] Magnum quippe et laudabile commercium relinquere temporalia pro eternis, promereri celestia pro terrenis, centuplum pro uno recipere, ac beatam vitam perpetuam possidere.

[31] Quapropter vestram excellenciam et sanctitatem duxi, prout possum, humilibus precibus *in Christi visceribus*[23] supplicandam, quatenus in eius sancto servicio confortari velitis, [32] crescentes de bono in melius, de virtutibus in virtutes, ut cui toto mentis desiderio deservitis, dignetur vobis optata premia elargiri.

[33] Obsecro etiam vos in Domino, sicut possum, ut me vestram famulam, licet inutilem, et sorores ceteras vobis devotas mecum in monasterio commorantes habere velitis in sanctissimis vestris oracionibus commendatas, [34] quibus subvenientibus mereri possimus misericordiam Ihesu Christi, ut pariter una vobiscum divina mereamur perfrui visione.

[35] Valete in Domino et oretis pro me.

---

23   Phil 1, 8.

[30] What a great and praiseworthy piece of business it is: to leave the temporal for the eternal; to be promised the heavenly in exchange for the earthly; to receive a hundred-fold in place of one; to possess the blessed, eternal life.

[31] This is why I have led Your Excellency and Your Holiness by offering such humble prayers as I am capable of in the bowels of Christ, so that [32] You may be strengthened in His holy service and also that You may grow from good to better and from strength to strength. Then He, to whom You are devoted with all the longing of Your mind, may deign to pour out on You the reward You long for.

[33] I also beg You in the Lord, as much as I possibly can, that in Your most holy prayers You remember both me, Your family servant (although an unprofitable one), and the other sisters in the monastery with me, who are as devoted to You as I am. [34] With this help, we may be able to merit the mercy of Jesus Christ so that equally with You we may also merit to rejoice in the eternal vision.

[35] Farewell in the Lord and pray for me.

Notes to the First Letter of St Clare to St Agnes

[a] In 1896 Achille Ratti, later Pope Pius IX, then Librarian in Milan, discovered a manuscript text of Clare's letters, which is the Latin version used here. These letters were analysed in 1932 by Jan Kapistran Vyskočil who concluded that the Milan manuscript had been copied in Prague between 1283 and 1322 or a little later. He suggested that the Milan text had been sent to Rome as part of the dossier put together when Agnes' canonisation was first petitioned, between 1332 and 1339. War and other political troubles then overwhelmed Bohemia and the matter was dropped.

[b] Clare sent Agnes four gifts: a wooden bowl to show she was a mendicant; a set of beads (not a rosary) for prayer; a black veil to signify her religious profession and a crucifix to show her following of Christ.

[c] Ottokar I (1198-1230)

[d] This is the only time Clare uses this phrase. At that time, *inclusa* and *reclusa* had slightly different meanings, the latter being nearer to what we would understand by 'solitude', the former to 'cloistered'.

[e] The capital You is retained because Clare is speaking formally.

[f] This refers to the Emperor Frederick II who married his third wife, Isabella of England in July 1235. Their second child, born and died in 1237, was called Agnes. These dates give a probable frame for this letter.

The Second Letter
of Saint Clare to
Saint Agnes of Prague

1234–1238

The Second Letter of St Clare to Saint Agnes

Context and Date

The letter belongs to Agnes' early years in religious life. She had entered the monastery and was now abbess, having been appointed by Pope Gregory IX to take effect on the day of her profession. As we read the letters and ponder Agnes' history, we can see her grow in understanding the call to most high poverty. Her nobility now comes from her relationship with Jesus Christ into whose service she has entered. This second letter was written somewhere during the years 1234 to 1238, as spiritual direction, formation, guidance and encouragement.

Theme

The greatness of God's generous gifts given to Agnes.

Things to note

Note the Latin with its typical mediaeval, phonetic spelling.

Note that Clare has moved from the formality of *vos* to the intimacy of *tu*, a significant shift.

The predominant number is five, recalling the five wounds of Jesus Christ.

Note the reference to Brother Elias. This was only a few years before his disgrace and the crash of 1239 but Clare clearly supports him as the successor of Francis and one who shares her vision, unlike Gregory IX with whom Agnes was discussing her vocation to poverty. It seems that Agnes' understanding of most high poverty developed gradually and Clare slowly led her deeper and deeper into the spirituality of it. So as Agnes understood more, she wanted more to commit herself to Clare's Form of Life and to petition Gregory for this. He was very reluctant to grant it and, in fact, Agnes was not to be successful for many years, not until the Protector of the Order, Rainaldo, became Pope Alexander IV in 1254.

[1] Filie Regis regum, ancille domini dominancium[1] sponse dignissime Ihesu Christi et ideo regine praenobili domine Agneti, [2] Clara, pauperum dominarum ancilla inutilis[2] et indigna salutem et semper in summa vivere paupertate.

[3] Gratias ago gratie largitori, a quo *omne datum optimum et omne datum perfectum*[3] creditur emanare, quod te tantis virtutum tytulis decoravit et tante perfectionis insigniis illustravit, [4] ut perfecti Patris[4] effecta diligens imitatrix, perfecta fieri merearis, ne oculi sui aliquid in te videant imperfectum.[5]

[5] Hec est illa perfectio, qua te sibi rex ipse in ethereo thalamo sociabit, ubi sedet stellato solio gloriosus [6] eo quod terreni regni fastigia vilipendens et oblationes imperialis coniugii parum dignans,

---

1   Rev 19,16; 1 Tim 6,15.
2   Lk 17,10.
3   Jas 1,17.
4   Cf. Eph 5,1.
5   Cf. Mt 5,48; Ps 139,16.

[1] To the daughter of the King of kings, to the handmaid of the Lord of lords, to the most worthy spouse of Jesus Christ[6] and therefore a most noble queen, to the Lady Agnes: [2] from Clare, an unprofitable and unworthy handmaid of the Poor Ladies: greetings, and may you always live in most high poverty.

[3] I give thanks to the generous Giver of grace from whom every best and perfect gift is believed to flow, for He has adorned you with the honour of such virtues and has made you illustrious with insignia of such perfection. [4] So that, being made a loving imitator of the Father of perfections, you might merit to be made perfect, lest His eyes should see anything in you which is imperfect.

[5] This is the perfection which the King Himself will share with you in the heavenly bridal chamber where He is gloriously seated on a throne of stars. [6] For you scorned as inadequate the offer of marriage to the Emperor (the pinnacle of an earthly kingdom)

---

6   AudPov 6.

[7] emula sanctissime paupertatis effecta, in spiritu magne humilitatis et ardentissime caritatis eius adhesisti vestigiis, cuius meruisti connubio copulari.

[8] Cum vero noverim te virtutibus oneratam, parcens prolixitati verborum nolo verbis superfluis onerare, [9] licet tibi nichil superfluum videatur ex hiis de quibus posset tibi aliqua consolacio provenire.

[10] Sed quia unum est necessarium,[7] hoc unum obtestor et moneo per amorem illius cui te sanctam et beneplacentem hostiam obtulisti, [11] ut, tui memor propositi, velud altera Rachel tuum semper videns principium, quod tenes teneas, quod facis facias nec dimittas, [12] sed cursu concito, gradu levi, pedibus inoffensis, ut etiam gressus tui pulverem non admittant, [13] secura, gaudens et alacris per tramitem caute beatitudinis gradiaris, [14] nulli credens, nulli

---

7   Lk 10,42; cf. Rom 12,1.

[7] being made, in the Spirit of great humility and most burning love, one who strives after most holy poverty, cleaving to the footprints[8] of Him to whom you have merited to be united as in marriage.

[8] Since I know that you are weighted with virtues, I will spare you an exuberance of words and will not give you the burden of superfluous ones [9] though I know nothing seems superfluous to you if it is able to bring you some consolation.

[10] Yet because one thing is necessary, I bear witness to that one thing. I admonish you, for love of Him to whom you have offered yourself as a holy and agreeable sacrifice, [11] like another Rachel, be mindful of your *propositum*[9] always looking to your beginning. What you hold now, may you always hold; what you are doing now, do without ceasing. [12] Instead, run even more swiftly, light-footed, treading carefully, so that your stepping raises no dust, [13] be sure-footed, joyful and swift on the path of blessedness, [14] believing nothing, agreeing

---

8   The Latin has *vestigia*, a word much used by Bonaventure, cf. 1 Pet 2, 21.

9   When Innocent III met members of the new poverty movements, he gave them a proto-Rule called a *propositum*. Clare is encouraging Agnes to persevere in that which Francis had given Clare as a *propositum*.

consenciens, quod te vellet ab hoc proposito revocare, quod tibi poneret in via scandalum ne in illa perfectione qua Spiritus Domini te vocavit,[10] *redderes Altissimo vota tua*.[11] [15] In hoc autem ut mandatorum Domini securius viam perambules, [12]venerabilis patris nostri fratris nostri Helye, generalis ministri consilium imitare; [16] quod prepone consiliis ceterorum et reputa tibi carius omni dono.

[17] Si quis vero aliud tibi dixerit, aliud tibi suggesserit quod perfectionem tuam impediat, quod vocacioni divine contrarium videatur, etsi debeas venerari, noli tamen eius consilium imitari, [18] sed pauperem Christum virgo pauper amplectere.

[19] Vide contemptibilem pro te factum et sequere, facta pro ipso contemptibilis in hoc mundo. [20] Sponsum tuum *prae filiis hominum speciosum*,[13] pro salute tua factum virorum vilissimum, despectum, percussum et toto corpore multipliciter flagellatum, inter ipsas crucis angustias morientem, regina praenobilis, intuere, considera, contemplare desiderans imitari.

---

10   Rom 14,13; Ps 50,14.
11   Ps 49,14.
12   Ps 118,32.
13   Ps 45,3; cf. Mt 27,26; Ps 44,3.

to nothing which would make you want to call this back, or which would place a stumbling block in your way. In that case, you would not be giving back your vows to the Most High in that perfection to which the Spirit of the Lord has called you. [15] In all this then, so that you may walk more securely along the way of the Lord's commands, follow the advice of our venerable Father, our Brother Elias, the Minister General. [16] Prefer this advice to that of any others and hold it dearer than any gift.

[17] If anyone says anything else to you, or suggests anything else to you which would hinder your perfection, or which seems to be against the divine call, although you must respect him, do not follow his advice, [18] but embrace the poor Christ, O poor virgin.

[19] See Him, made contemptible for you and follow, being made contemptible for Him in this world. [20] Your Bridegroom, who is the most beautiful of the sons of humanity, for your salvation was made the most vile of men, despised, beaten and many times whipped all over His whole body, dying on the cross in the depths of anguish. O most noble queen, gaze, consider, contemplate, longing to imitate.

[21] Cui si *compateris*[14] *conregnabis,*[15] condolens *congaudebis*[16], in cruce tribulationes *commoriens,*[17] cum ipso *in sanctorum spendoribus*[18] mansiones ethereas possidebis,

[22] et *nomen* tuum *in libro vite*[19] notabitur, futurum inter homines gloriosum. [23] Propter quod in eternum et in seculum seculi regni celestis gloriam pro terrenis et transitoriis, eterna bona pro perituris percipies et vives in secula seculorum.

[24] Vale, carissima soror, et domina propter Dominum tuum sponsum, [25] et me cum sororibus meis, que gaudemus de bonis Domini, que in te per suam graciam operatur, stude tuis devotis orationibus Domino commendare. [26] Sororibus eciam tuis nos plurimum recommenda.

---

14   1 Cor 12,26.
15   2 Tim 2,12.
16   1 Cor 12,26.
17   2 Tim 2,11.
18   Ps 109,3.
19   Phil 4,3; Rev 3,5.

[21] If you suffer with Him, then you will reign with Him; grieving with Him, then you will rejoice with Him; dying with Him on the cross of torments, then you will possess heavenly mansions with Him in the splendour of the saints.

[22] Your name will be noted in the Book of Life, and among men and women you will have a glorious future. [23] This is why in eternity and for ever and ever, you will share in the glory of the heavenly Kingdom instead of an earthly and transient one. You will live for ever and ever in an everlasting good, instead of a good which will perish.

[24] Farewell, dearest Sister and Lady because of the Lord your Spouse. [25] Work hard in your devout prayers at recommending me and my sisters to the Lord, so that we may rejoice in the good[a] of the Lord which by His grace is at work in you. [26] We also recommend ourselves to your sisters over and over again.

Secunda Epistola

Notes to the Second Letter of St Clare
to St Agnes

[a] The 'good' or the *bonum* is a key element in the theology of both Bonaventure and Scotus. We know that Bonaventure went to Leo to learn about Clare's spirituality and way of life and here we see Clare expressing something to which Francis had opened her eyes and which those two scholars later developed into a remarkable Franciscan theology.

The Third Letter
of Saint Clare to
Saint Agnes of Prague

1238

The Third Letter of Saint Clare to Saint Agnes

Context and Date

It is clear from this letter that Agnes had asked advice from Clare about fasting. The background is Gregory IX's imposition on all the women's communities of Cistercian style fasting and abstinence. Once again we find Clare basically saying: attend to Francis, not Gregory who offers a different charism (as we would say). Gregory's letter is *Licet velut ignis* of 9 February 1238 (BF I, p. 209).

Theme

The theme is one of strong encouragement, not so much to conversion as to endurance and perseverance. Clare encourages Agnes and insists that she is doing wonderfully well and can take courage to continue along the path she is already travelling. In December of this year 1238, Gregory IX wrote to Agnes's abbess (Agnes was no longer abbess at this point) insisting on the fasting prescribed in his Constitutions, though Agnes had asked, almost verbatim for the fasting described here by Clare as that worked out with Francis. It is almost impossible to say whether Clare or Gregory wrote first, unfortunately.

Things to note

The letter falls into two distinct halves, one of encouragement and praise, and the other of information about fasting.

Letter by letter we see their relationship growing and deepening. The fourth letter which is one of farewell will bring this to a crescendo.

In this letter we find Clare's first exposition of the theme of the mirror. This was a common image in the Middle Ages and, although not original to Clare, we can see that she made it her own on a deep level. The imagery is not quite consistent when we try to imagine it in physical terms, and we need to bear in mind that the word *speculum* meant both a mirror and an outstanding example. Here we find both meanings in function.

Note the accuracy of Clare's theology; she knows we come to the mirror of eternity (not eternity itself), to the splendour of the glory (not the glory itself), the figure of the divine substance (not the divinity itself). All these images, of course, refer to Christ who is Himself the mirror of the Father, the splendour of God's glory, the figure or image of the divine substance.

Theologians are not happy with her words 'through contemplation transform *yourself*'. Clare was no Pelagian, pulling herself up to heaven by her own bootlaces, but is speaking about our essential option for and surrender to the work of grace, and above all the work of contemplation. We choose to give time and energy and our very selves to the work of contemplation, and thereby open ourselves to transformation, however painful. By stepping into the light we transform ourselves, though we know well that it is the light which transforms. This seems to be the line of Clare's thought here. She is offering us a method of prayer which we may reasonably understand to describe her own prayer as well.

About fasting, she stands firmly on the instructions of Francis. Although stricter than Francis on fasting, she was, as always, ready to adapt to individual needs and capabilities – though not always to her own! Gregory's imposition of Cistercian fasting and abstinence was very hard for communities like Clare's and Agnes' which relied very much on what was given them in the way of food. Also the winters in Prague were very hard and Agnes had asked Gregory for clarifications in the light of this.

[1] In Christo sibi reverendissime domine ac pre cunctis mortalibus diligende sorori Agneti, illustris regis Bohemie germane, sed iam summo celorum regi[1] sorori et sponse, [2] Clara humillima et indigna Christi ancilla et dominarum pauperum serva, salutis gaudia in auctore salutis[2] et quidquid melius desiderari potest.

[3] De sospitate tua, felici statu et successibus prosperis quibus te in incepto cursu ad obtinendum celeste bravium[3] vigere intelligo tanto repleor gaudio [4] tantaque in Domino exultacione respiro, quanto te novi et arbitror vestigiorum pauperis et humilis Ihesu Christi tam in me quam in ceteris nostris sororibus imitationis mirifice supplere defectum.

[5] Vere gaudere possum, nec me aliquis posset a tanto gaudio facere alienam, [6] cum, quod sub celo concupivi iam tenens, callidi hostis astucias et perditricem humane nature superbiam et vanitatem humana corda infatuantem te quadam mirabili ipsius Dei oris sapientie prerogativa suffultam, terribiliter ac inopinabiliter videam supplantare,[4]

---

1   Mt 12, 50; cf. 2 Cor 11, 2.
2   Heb 2, 10; cf. Phil 4, 8-9.
3   Phil 3, 14; 1 Cor 9, 24.
4   Cf. Song 3, 3; Gen 3, 1.

[1] To the Lady whom, in Christ, she most respects; to her sister Agnes whom she loves more than any other mortal, to the blood-sister of the illustrious King of Bohemia but now the sister and bride[5] of the most high King of the heavens: [2] from Clare, the most lowly and unworthy handmaid of Christ and the serf[a] of the Poor Ladies; the joy of salvation in the author of salvation and whatever better thing there is that can be desired.

[3] From your good health, your happiness and the good outcome you are achieving in the race for the heavenly prize which you have begun so vigorously,[b] I am all the more filled with delight;[6] [4] and the more I know and can see that you are following the vestiges of the poor and humble Jesus Christ, the greater is the exultation I breathe in the Lord, for you are wonderfully making up what is lacking in me as much as the other sisters.

[5] Truly I can rejoice, nor can anyone alienate me from such joy, [6] since what I had desired under heaven, I am already holding. I see that you are sustained by the wonderful privilege of wisdom[c] from the mouth of God Himself; that you have overthrown the shrewdness of the astute enemy in an awe-inspiring and unexpected way,

---

5   1LtF 6-12.
6   TestCL 23.

[7] absconsumque in agro mundi et cordium humanorum thesaurum incomparabilem,[7] quo id emitur a quo cuncta de nichilo facta sunt[8], humilitate, virtute fidei ac paupertatis brachiis amplexari [8] et, ut proprie ipsius apostoli verbis utar, ipsius Dei te iudico *adiutricem*[9] et ineffabilis corporis eius cadencium membrorum sublevatricem. [9] Quis ergo de tantis mirandis gaudiis dicat me non gaudere?[10] [10] Gaudeas igitur et tu in Domino semper,[11] carissima, [11] nec te involvat amaritudo et nebula, o in Christo dilectissima domina, angelorum gaudium et corona sororum.[12]

[12] Pone mentem tuam in speculo eternitatis, pone animam tuam in splendore glorie,[13] [13] pone cor tuum in figura divine substantie, et transforma te ipsam totam per contemplacionem in ymagine divinitatis ipsius, [14] ut et ipsa sencias quod senciunt amici gustando absconditam dulcedinem quam ipse Deus ab inicio suis amatoribus reservavit.[14]

---

7   Cf. Mt 13, 44; Lk 1, 51.
8   Cf. Jn 1, 3.
9   1 Cor 3, 9.
10   Rom 16, 3.
11   Phil 4, 4.
12   Cf. Phil 4, 1.
13   Cf.. Heb 1, 3; cf.. 2 Cor 3, 18.
14   Cf. Ps 30, 20; cf. 1 Cor 2, 9

and you have overthrown the pride which destroys
human nature[15] and the vanity which infatuates the
human heart
[7] An incomparable treasure is hidden in the field of the
world and in the human heart. With it, that by which
everything was made from nothing has been bought.
You have embraced it, by humility, by the power of faith
and by the arms of poverty. [8] And, to use the very
words of the Apostle, I judge you to be a co-worker of
God Himself and one who supports from beneath[d] those
members of His ineffable Body who are giving way. [9]
Who then could tell me not to rejoice at such wonderful
joys?[16] [10] Therefore you too, my dearest, rejoice in the
Lord always, [11] and may neither bitterness nor clouds
overwhelm you, most beloved Lady in Christ, joy of the
angels and crown of the sisters.

[12] So place your mind in the mirror of eternity, place
your soul in the splendour of glory.[17] [13] Place your
heart in the figure of the divine substance and, through
contemplation, transform your whole self into an image
of the Godhead.[18] [14] Do this so that you too may feel
what His friends feel on tasting the hidden sweetness

---

15   2Reg 22, 20.
16   Cf. v. 5.
17   TestCl 19-21.
18   Adm 5, 1; 2Reg, 23, 3.

[15] Et omnibus que in hoc fallaci mundo perturbabili suos cecos amatores[19] illaqueant penitus pretermissis, illum totaliter diligas qui se totum pro tua dilectione donavit, [16] cuius pulchritudinem sol et luna mirantur, cuius premiorum preciositas incomparabilis et eorum *magnitudinis non est finis,*[20] illum [17] dico altissimi Dei filium, quem virgo peperit et post cuius partum virgo permansit. [18] Ipsius dulcissime matri adhereas, que talem genuit filium quem celi capere non poterant,[21] [19] et tamen ipsa parvulo claustro sacri uteri contulit et gremio puellari gestavit.

[20] Quis non abhorreat humani hostis insidias, qui per fastum momentaneorum et fallacium gloriarum ad nichilum redigere cogit quod maius est celo? [21] Ecce iam liquet per Dei graciam dignissimam creaturarum fidelis hominis animam maiorem esse quam celum, [22] cum celi cum creaturis ceteris capere nequeant creatorem, et sola fidelis anima ipsius mansio sit et sedes, et hoc solum per caritatem qua carent impii,

---

19   Cf. Gal, 2, 20.
20   Ps 144, 3; cf. Jn 14, 23.
21   1 Kings 8, 27; 2 Chron 2, 5.

which God has kept from the beginning for those who love Him.

[15] And completely passing over all those things with which an untrustworthy and disturbed world entangles its blind lovers, love totally the One who gave His whole self for your love, [16] the One at whose beauty the sun and moon wonder,[22] the One whose rewards – with their value and greatness – have no end. [17] I am speaking about the One who is the Son of the Most High, whom the Virgin brought to birth and remained a virgin after His birth.[23] [18] Cleave to His most sweet Mother who begot such a Son as the heavens cannot contain,[24] [19] and yet she received Him into the small confines of her holy womb and she held Him on her young girl's lap.

[20] Who would not shrink from being ambushed by humanity's enemy[25] which, with the pride of a momentary and false glory, schemes to reduce to nothing something which is greater than the heavens? [21] How obvious it is that through the grace of God the faithful human soul,[26] that most worthy creation, is far greater than the heavens.

---

22   Feast of St Agnes, 21 January, Matins.
23   Feast of the Annunciation, 25 March, Matins.
24   SalV 4-6.
25   RegEr 6.
26   2Reg 22, 27; 1LtF 10, 5.

[23] veritate dicente: *Qui diligit me diligetur a Patre meo*[27] *et ego diligam eum et ad eum veniemus et mansionem apud eum faciemus.*[28]

[24] Sicut ergo virgo virginum gloriosa materialiter, [25] sic et tu, *sequens eius vestigia*[29] humilitatis presertim et paupertatis, casto et virgineo pectore spiritualiter semper sine dubietate omni portare potes, [26] illum *continens* a quo et tu et *omnia continentur,*[30] id possidens quod, et comparate cum ceteris huius mundi possessionibus transeuntibus, forcius possidetur.

[27] In quo quidam mundani reges et regine falluntur, [28] quorum superbie usque ad celum licet ascenderint et capita eorum nubes tetigerint, quasi sterquilinium in fine perduntur.[31]

[29] Super hiis autem que me iam reserare mandasti, [30] que scilicet essent festa que forte, ut te opinor aliquatenus estimasse in varietate ciborum gloriosissimus pater noster sanctus Franciscus nos celebrare specialiter monuisset, caritati tue duxi respondendum.

---

27   Jn 14, 21, 23.
28   Jn 14, 23.
29   1 Pet 2, 21.
30   Wis 1, 7; Col, 1, 17.
31   Cf. Is, 14, 11-15; Job 20, 6-7.

[22] The heavens together with all other creatures cannot contain the Creator. Only the faithful soul^e itself is His mansion and His throne, and this only through love – which the ungodly lack [23] Truth itself has said: Those who love Me will be loved by My Father and I shall love him, and we will come to him and make our home with him.

[24] Just as the glorious Virgin of virgins materially, [25] so you too spiritually will certainly be able to carry Him in your chaste and virginal body by following in her vestiges[32] (especially those of humility and poverty).[33] [26] You will contain Him by whom you and everything are contained, possessing that which – in comparison with other transitory possessions – you will possess more completely.

[27] In this, certain kings and queens of the world are mistaken.[34] [28] Though their pride climbs right to the skies and their heads touch the clouds, in the end they will vanish like manure.

[29] Now, about those things you asked me to open up for you [30] to let you know which are the feasts that our most glorious Father Saint Francis urged us specially to

---

32 *Vestiges,* meaning footprints or traces, is used here because it became a key word for Bonaventure.

33 1Reg 9, 1; 2LtF 63; TestCl, 46; LtLeo 3.

34 1LtF 12, 4, 7; RegEr 6.

[31] Noverit quidem tua prudencia, quod, preter debiles et infirmas, quibus de quibuscumque cibariis omnem discrecionem quam possemus facere nos monuit et mandavit, [32] nulla nostrum sana existens et valida nisi cibaria quadragesimalia tantum, tam in diebus ferialibus quam festivis manducare deberet, die quolibet ieiunando, [33] demptis diebus dominicis et die natalis Domini, in quibus bis in die comedere deberemus, [34] et in diebus quoque yovis solitis temporibus, pro voluntate cuiuslibet, ut que scilicet nollet ieiunare non teneretur.

[35] Nos tamen sane ieiunamus cottidie preter dies dominicos et natalis.

[36] In omni vero pascha, ut scriptum beati Francisci dicit, et festivitatibus sancte Marie ac sanctorum apostolorum ieiunare eciam non tenemur, nisi hec festa in sexta feria evenirent.

[37] Et, sicut predictum est, semper que sane sumus et valide, cibaria quadragesimalia manducamus.

celebrate[35] by some variation in the food. I think you already know this but I am prompted to respond because of your love. [31] In your prudence you should know that apart from the weak and infirm (for whom he counselled us – and commanded us – that in the matter of food we use our judgement as far as possible)[36] [32] we who are healthy and strong enough should only eat Lenten fare.[37] This is for ferial or feast days, so we fast every day [33] except Sundays and the Birth of the Lord.[38] Then we should eat twice in the day. [34] Normally on Thursdays in Ordinary Time each one may choose. She who does not want to fast is not obliged to.

[35] However, we who are healthy fast daily except on Sundays and Christmas Day.
[36] For the whole of Easter, as the writing of Blessed Francis says, and on the feasts of holy Mary and the holy Apostles, we are not obliged to fast unless those feasts fall on a Friday;
[37] and as I said before, we who are healthy and strong enough should always eat Lenten food.

---

35   RegCl 3, 8-11.
36   RegCl 3, 10.
37   RegCl 3, 8.
38   RegCl 3, 9.

[38] Verum quia *nec caro* nostra *caro enea est nec fortitudo lapidis fortitudo*[39] nostra [39] ymmo fragiles et omni corporali sumus debilitati proclive, [40] a quadam indiscreta et impossibili abstiencie austeritate quam te aggressam esse cognovi, sapienter, carissima, et discrete te retrahi rogo et in Domino peto.

[41] ut *vivens vivens confiteris Domino,*[40] *rationabile tuum* reddas *obsequium*[41] et *tuum sacrificium*[42] semper *sale conditum.*[43]

[42] Vale semper in Domino, sicut me valere peropto, et tam me quam meas sorores tuis sacris sororibus recommendes.

---

39   Job 6, 12.
40   Is 38, 19; Sir 17, 27.
41   Rom 12, 1.
42   Is 38, 19; cf. Sir 17, 27; Rom 12, 1.
43   Lev 2, 13; Col 4, 6, Job 6, 6; Lev 2, 13; Col 4, 6.

[38] It is true that our flesh is not the flesh of bronze nor is our strength the strength of stone.[44] [39] On the contrary, we are fragile and prone to every bodily weakness,[45] [40] and for that very reason I beg you, my dearest, to back away from that indiscreet and impossible austerity of abstinence which I know you have undertaken with ferocity. And in the Lord, I ask

[41] that living, you live to praise the Lord, that you give back to the Lord your reasonable homage and that your sacrifice be always seasoned with salt.

[42] May you always have strength in the Lord as I very much hope I shall always have strength, and may you recommend[46] both me and my sisters to your holy sisters.

---

44   1LtF 10, 2; RegCl 6, 2; TestCl 27.
45   1LtF 1, 5.
46   2LtAg 26.

Notes to the Third Letter of St Clare to St Agnes

[a] In the other letters Clare speaks of herself as the handmaid, *ancilla*, of the sisters, but here she uses this much stronger word, *serva*, imitating Christ Himself who humbled Himself and took the form of a slave. 'Serf' is a powerful word to use for *serva* but more accurately translates Clare's extreme statement. It gains further impact in being addressed to a former princess of Bohemia. In the other letters, Clare calls herself the handmaid, *ancilla* to the sisters. Here we see poverty lived out in practice and Clare's insight that it means a great deal more than material want. In these opening verses, she has clearly placed Agnes' earthly descent within the context of her new spiritual relationships. Note too that in Matthew 24, it is the servant who prepares the food – is this also an introduction to a letter about fasting?

[b] Clare wastes no time in bringing in images of struggle. She will develop these throughout the letter, especially in this first part where she is encouraging Agnes to be steadfast in her struggle to live most high poverty. There is a progression in Clare's thought: in LtAg 1, 14-17, poverty is embraced; in LtAg 2, 7 she is wed; here she is to be taken hold of, grasped.

^c In his letter *De conditoris omnium*, 9 May 1238, Gregory likens Agnes to the Queen of the South who came seeking the wisdom of Solomon. Clare picks up on this and says that Agnes is receiving wisdom directly from the Most High. In verses 6, 12 and 20, Clare echoes Gregory's letter and much insight is to be gained by comparing the two texts. Gregory's letter is an extraordinarily fulsome way of saying that she should accept his Constitutions instead of the Form of Life which Francis gave to Clare (as Agnes was petitioning). It is only in a further letter two days later that he spells it out more specifically (*Angelis gaudium*, 11 May 1238).

^d The Latin word is *sublevatrix*, and the implication is that because Agnes has found the treasure of poverty hidden in the field of the heart, she is now able to lift up all others, no matter how poor and humiliated. There is nobody she cannot now reach. We know that Agnes' monastery was a most generous resource for the poor of Bohemia, and the huge bread oven in the courtyard to this day indicates that their giving to the poor was on a considerable scale.

^e The faithful soul was a phrase used by the early Franciscans, see both Letters to the Faithful as well as the *Sacrum Commercium*, The Holy Exchange, and Clare unambiguously means the soul who is faithful

to the *propositum* of *sine proprio.* This is the fidelity in question, not the issue of fasting, and through this fidelity we are filled with grace and become his dwelling place in fulfilment of Jesus' promise in John 14, 21.

The Fourth Letter
of Saint Clare to
Saint Agnes of Prague

1253

The Fourth Letter of Saint Clare to Saint Agnes

Context and date

This is Clare's last letter to Agnes, a letter of farewell in which Clare tries to express her love for her sister and to share with her (and us) how thin is the boundary between this world and the next. In the light of her words, we can accurately date it to 1253.

Theme

The theme is the fulfilment in God of all our human love. The Spirit takes our loves and transforms them into something unutterably beautiful, intense and eternal.

Things to note

Note the intensity of Clare's language and how unafraid she is of her feelings and of her love for Agnes. The whole tone of this letter is a remarkable blend of intensity and serenity. She focuses Agnes on the future and the goal of all her struggle – to follow the Lamb (*Agnus* in Latin) wherever he goes. Clare is leaving Agnes with all the reassurance she can, knowing that Agnes will now have to lead the struggle for the Form of Life. She is handing on the torch, as it were. Clare's own sister Agnes of Assisi would be a strong support but she was not a leader as

Agnes of Prague clearly was. Also we know that Agnes of Assisi died the following November.

Note the predominance of the number seven – the number of perfection, and the way it occasionally tips into eight, which signified the next world, perfection and then one more. Clare gives Agnes seven titles in the very first verse, setting the scene as it were.

The lack of messengers which she mentions (v. 6) was primarily due to the Pope-Emperor conflict which kept Italy and especially the Papal States in turmoil with armies marching up and down, mercenaries abounding, changing sides according to the pay and all the chaos that attends war. We may also see here a reference to the way the authorities of the Friars Minor had distanced themselves from Clare, since she was such a staunch promoter of the way of life which Francis had given her in the beginning, while the friars were in rapid development to meet the needs of the Church. Clare never made any criticism of this but continued to 'do what was hers to do' as Francis had taught. Gregory needed political support from Agnes' brother the King of Bohemia, so she was not as easily silenced as Clare. So Clare binds Agnes to the cause with strong bands of love.

Set into the letter (vv. 9-14) is another of the troubadour style songs which we have seen in earlier letters. They repay study as poetry and song and may even have been used liturgically. There is no reason to doubt that they are by Clare; it should not surprise us that so close an associate of Francis would herself be a poet and singer of songs.

[1] Anime sue dimidio et precordialis amoris armarie singulari, illustri regine Agni regis eterni sponse domine Agneti, matri sue carissime ac filie sue inter omnes alias speciali, [2] Clara, indigna Christi famula et ancilla inutilis[1] ancillarum eius commorantium in monasterio sancti Damiani de Assisio, [3] salutem et cum reliquis sanctissimis virginibus *ante thronum* Dei et Agni *novum cantare canticum et quocumque ierit Agnum sequi.[2]*

[4] O mater et filia,[3] sponsa regis omnium seculorum, et si tibi non scripsi frequenter, prout anima tua et mea pariter desiderat et peroptat, aliquatenus ne mireris, [5] nec credas ullatenus incendium caritatis erga te minus ardere suaviter in visceribus matris tue. [6] Hoc est, impediverunt defectus nunciorum et viarum pericula manifesta.

[7] Nunc vero scribens caritati tue, congaudeo et exulto tibi in gaudio spiritus,[4] sponsa Christi, [8] quia velut altera virgo sanctissima sancta Agnes *Agno* immaculato[5] *qui tollit peccata mundi[6]* es mirifice desponsata, spretis omnibus vanitatibus huius mundi.

---

1   Lk 17, 10.
2   Apoc 14, 3-4.
3   Cf. Mt 12, 50; cf. 2 Cor 11, 2.
4   1 Thess 1, 6.
5   1 Pet 1, 19.
6   Jn 1, 29.

[1] To the half of her soul and the special shrine of her heart's intimate love, to the illustrious Queen, to the Bride of the eternal King, to the Lady Agnes, her dearest mother and the daughter who is special among all the others; [2] Clare, the unworthy family servant of Christ[7] and the unprofitable handmaid of His handmaids who abide in the monastery of San Damiano in Assisi: greetings. [3] With the rest of the holy virgins may she sing the new song before the throne of God and of the Lamb. May she follow the Lamb wherever He goes.[a]

[4] O mother and daughter,[8] bride of the King of all ages, although I have not written to you very often, and not as much as your soul and mine equally desire – and very much wish for as well – do not be surprised. [5] And do not believe, either, that therefore the fire of love for you burns any less sweetly in the bowels of your mother.[9] [6] This is the hindrance: the lack of messengers and the obvious dangers of the roads.

[7] However, now that I am writing to you, dearest, I rejoice and exult with you in the joy of the Spirit, O Bride of Christ, [8] because you, like that other most holy virgin Saint Agnes, are wonderfully wedded to the

---

7   RegCl 1, 3; 10, 6; TestCl 37; BlCl 5.
8   1LtF 10, 6-12; RegCl 6, 3; 1LtAg 12, 24; 3LtAg 1.
9   RegCl 8, 16; TestCl 63.

[9] Felix certe cui hoc sacro datur potiri connubio, ut ei adhereatur totis cordis precordiis,[10]

[10] cuius pulchritudinem omnia beata celorum agmina incessabiliter admirantur,[11]
[11] cuius affectus afficit, cuius contemplatio reficit, cuius implet benignitas,

[12] cuius replet suavitas, cuius memoria lucescit suaviter,
[13] *cuius odore mortui reviviscent[12]* cuiusque visio gloriosa beatificabit omnes cives superne Iherusalem,[13]

[14] qui, *cum sit splendor glorie[14]* et *candor lucis eterne*, est *speculum sine macula.[15]*

[15] Hoc speculum cottidie intuere, o regina et sponsa Ihesu Christi, et in eo faciem tuam iugiter speculare,[16]

---

10   Lk 14, 15; Apoc 19, 9.
11   1 Pt 1, 12.
12   Passion of St. Agnes the Roman Martyr.
13   Apoc 21, 2-10; Gal 4, 26.
14   Heb 1, 3.
15   Wis 7, 26; Apoc 21, 11-23.
16   2 Cor 11:2.

spotless Lamb who takes away the sins of the world, for you have laid aside all the vanities of this world.

[9] She is certainly happy
who has been given to drink at this banquet
in order to cleave with all her heart to Him,
[10] at whose beauty all the blessed hosts of heaven
unceasingly wonder,[17]
[11] whose love stirs to love,
whose contemplation remakes,
whose kindliness floods,
[12] whose sweetness fills,
whose memory glows gently,
[13] whose fragrance brings the dead to life again,
the glorious vision of whom
will make all the citizens of the Jerusalem above
most blessed,
[14] He is the splendour of eternal glory,
the brightness of everlasting light
and an unspotted mirror.

[15] Gaze into this mirror every day, O Queen, Bride of Jesus Christ,[18] and constantly see your own face reflected in it,[b]

---

17   LtLeo 7, 9.
18   TestCl 19-21.

[16] ut sic totam interius et exterius te adornes, amictam *circumdatamque varietatibus¹⁹* [17] omnium virtutum floribus et vestimentis pariter adornatam, sicut decet filiam et sponsam carissimam summi regis.²⁰

[18] In hoc autem speculo refulget beata paupertas, sancta humilitas et ineffabilis caritas, sicut per totum speculum poteris cum Dei gracia contemplari.

[19] Attende, inquam, principium huius speculi, paupertatem positi siquidem in presepio²¹ et in panniculis involuti. [20] O miranda humilitas, o stupenda paupertas: [21] rex angelorum, dominus celi et terre²² in presepio reclinatur.²³
[22] In medio autem speculi considera humilitatem sanctam, beatam paupertatem, labores innumeros ac penalitates quas sustinuit pro redemptione humani generis.
[23] In fine vero eiusdem speculi contemplare ineffabilem caritatem qua pati voluit in crucis stipite et in eodem mori omni mortis genere turpiori.

---

19   Ps 44, 10.
20   Ps 44, 11-12.
21   Lk 2, 12.
22   Cf. Mt. 11, 25.
23   Lk 2, 7.

[16] so that you may adorn your whole being, within and without,^c in richly decorated robes. [17] Adorn yourself, as is only fitting, with virtues like flowers, and garments every bit as ornate as those of the daughter and dearly beloved Bride of the Most High King.

[18] For in that mirror shine blessed poverty, holy humility, love beyond words as – by the grace of God – you can contemplate in the whole mirror.

[19] Turn your mind, I say, to the border of this mirror; to the poverty of Him who was placed in a manger[24] and wrapped in tiny garments.[25] [20] O wonderful humility! O astounding poverty![26] [21] The King of Angels, the Lord of heaven and earth, rests in a manger. [22] Then in the centre of the mirror, consider the holy humility, not to speak of the blessed poverty,[27] the infinite and costly troubles which He took upon Himself to redeem the human race.
[23] At the edges of that same mirror, contemplate the love beyond words through which He chose to suffer on the Tree of the cross and, on that same Tree, to die the most disgraceful death of any.

---

24   Gregory IX, *Pia credulitate tenentes*, 15 April 1238, BF I, 236.
25   RegCl 2, 25; ClTest 45.
26   2LtF 34-35.
27   Adm 6, 1.

[24] Unde ipsum speculum, in ligno crucis positum, ad hec consideranda transeuntes monebat dicens: [25] *O vos omnes qui transitis per viam, attendite et videte si est dolor similis sicut dolor meus.*[28]

[26] Respondeamus ei clamanti et eiulanti una voce, uno spiritu: *Memoria memor ero et tabescet in me anima mea.*[29] [27] Huius igitur caritatis ardore accendaris iugiter forcius, o regina celestis regis.

[28] Contemplans insuper indicibiles eius delicias, divicias et honores perpetuos [29] et suspirando pre nimio cordis desiderio et amore proclames: [30] *Trahe me post te, curremus in odorem unguentorum tuorum*[30] sponse celestis.

[31] Curram nec deficiam, donec *introducas me in cellam vinariam,*[31] donec [32] *leva* tua sit *sub capite meo et dextera* tua feliciter *amplexetur me, osculeris me* felicissimo tui *oris osculo.*[32]

---

28   Lam 1, 12.
29   Lam 3, 20.
30   Song 1, 2-3.
31   Song 2, 4.
32   Song 2, 6; 8, 3; 1, 1.

[24] Therefore, when it was placed on the wood of the cross, that same mirror taught the one who passed by to consider all this, saying: [25] O all you who pass by the way, look and see if there is any sorrow like my sorrow! [26] Let us respond to Him with one voice, one spirit, crying out and grieving: 'I hold this memory in my mind and my spirit faints within me.' [27] So may you always catch fire more and more strongly from this burning love, O Queen of the heavenly King![33]

[28] Over and above this, contemplating His inexpressible delights, riches and everlasting honours, [29] and sighing with the immense longing and love in your heart, may you cry out: [30] O heavenly Bridegroom, draw me after you and we will run in the fragrance of your perfumes![d]

[31] I will run without stopping
until You lead me into the wine cellar,
[32] until Your left arm be under my head
and Your right will happily embrace me,
You will kiss me
with the happiest kiss of Your mouth.

---

33   AudPov 6.

[33] In hac contemplacione posita, habeas memoriam pauercule matris tuae, [34] sciens quod ego tuam felicem memoriam descripsi inseparabiliter *in tabulis cordis*³⁴ mei, habens te pre omnibus cariorem.³⁵

[35] Quid plura? Sileat in dilectione tua lingua carnis et loquatur lingua spiritus. [36] O filia benedicta, quoniam dilectionem quam ad te habeo nullatenus posset exprimere plenius lingua carnis, [37] que semiplene scripsi oro benigne ac devote suscipias, attendens in eis saltem affectum maternum quo circa te ac filias tuas caritatis ardore afficior omni die, quibus me ac filias meas in Christo plurimum recommenda.

[38] Ipse vero filie mee, sed precipue virgo prudentissima Agnes, soror nostra, se tibi et filiabus tuis, quantum possunt recommendant.

[39] Vale, carissima filia, cum filiabus tuis usque ad thronum glorie magni Dei et orate pro nobis.³⁶

---

34   Prov 3, 3.
35   2 Cor 3, 3.
36   Titus 2, 13; cf. 1 Thess 5:25.

[33] Being placed in this contemplation, keep the memory of your poor little mother, [34] knowing that I have inscribed the happy memory of you ineradicably on the tablets of my heart, holding you dearer than all others.

[35] What more? Let the tongue of the flesh be silent in loving you. Let that love be spoken by the tongue of the Spirit, [36] O blessed daughter, because love such as I have for you can never be expressed in its fullness by the tongue of the flesh. [37] It could be said that I have written the half of it. I beg you to receive it generously and lovingly.[37] Hear in it at least the motherly affection[38] through which I daily feel the flame of love for you and your daughters, and to whom, over and over again, I recommend myself and my daughters in Christ.

[38] In fact these same daughters of mine, and especially the most prudent virgin Agnes, our sister, recommend themselves in the Lord to you and to your daughters as much as they can.

[39] Farewell dearest daughter, together with your daughters, until the throne the glory of the great God, and pray for us.

---

37   TestCl 63.
38   LtLeo 2.

[40] Latores presencium carissimos nostros fratrem Amatum, *dilectum* utique *Deo et hominibus*[39] carum, et fratrem Bonaguram caritati tue quantum possum, presentibus recommendo. Amen.

---

39   Sir 45, 1.

[40] By this letter, I recommend to your love as much as I can the bearers of this letter, our dearest Brother Amatus (beloved by God and men) and our dearest Brother Bonagura. Amen.

Notes to the Fourth Letter of St Clare
to St Agnes

[a] Agnes, the Roman Martyr, was one of the great
models for mediaeval women and the patron of Agnes
of Prague. Here and in other places in her letters, Clare
links these two together by playing on the Latin word
agnus, or lamb as one of the titles of Christ. It is possible
that this letter was written during Eastertide in 1253,
only a few months before Clare's death, as it echoes
the Easter liturgy which is filled with references to the
Apocalypse and to Christ, Lamb of God.

[b] This passage, 15-34, can be read as a demonstration of
ways of prayer: 15-17 represent *lectio*, reading the text
or gazing at the mirror; 18-23 are *meditatio,* meditation
or thinking about what we have read; 24-27 are *oratio,*
praying about it, the beginning of the journey from
head to heart; 28-34 are *contemplatio,* contemplation,
the prayer of the heart.

[c] Within and without seems to have been another key
insight of the early Franciscans. Celano tells us (1Cel
95, 2Cel 211) that Francis was wounded 'within
and without' by the stigmata, and Francis himself
in Admonition 24 speaks about the need for inner
contrition to express itself outwardly in penance.
Their concern was integrity in its fullest sense. Clare is
speaking out of this same line of thought.

^d Whether Clare intended it or not, there is a wonderful statement of the apostolic fruitfulness of contemplation in this sentence: Draw *me* and *we* run. As you draw me, so others are drawn with me for we are all one and nothing the contemplative does is without its consequences for others.

Ermentrude of Bruges

Ermentrude was the daughter of the mayor of Cologne. In 1240 she went on pilgrimage and finally settled in Bruges where she lived as a hermit for some twelve years. During that time she heard about Clare and they corresponded. So when Ermentrude set off again on pilgrimage to Rome, she made a detour to Assisi to visit Clare, only to find that Clare had died just two weeks before. However, she clearly talked with the sisters and, on returning to Bruges, changed her hermitage into a house of Poor Sisters. She later founded other communities in Flanders. Beyond that, little is known except that in the supplement to Wadding's *Annales Minorum* for 1257, Melissano de Macro indicates that Clare wrote at least two letters to Ermentrude.

The present text does not seem to be the original but is perhaps somebody else's substantial condensation of two letters. The vocabulary is very different from that of the other letters, for one thing, as is also the style.[1] However the tradition that Clare wrote to Ermentrude is strong although the text which we now have cannot be regarded as Clare's actual words to Ermentrude.

---

[1] Cf. D. De Kok, 'De Origine Ordinis S. Clarae in Flandria' in *AFH* 7 (1914) pp. 234-246.

Epistola ad Ermentrudem

[1] Ermentrudi sorori carissimae Clara Assisisias humilis ancilla Jesu Christi, salutem et pacem.
[2] Novi te, O carissima soror, mundi e caeno, opitulante gratia Dei, feliciter aufugisse; [3] quamobrem gaudeo et congratulor tibi ac iterum gaudeo te semitas virtutis cum tuis filiabus strenue calcare.

[4] Esto, carissima, fidelis ei
cui promisisti usque ad mortem,
ab eodem enim *coronaberis* laurea *vitae.*[2]

[5] Brevis est *labor* hic noster
at *merces* aeterna;[3]
non te confundant strepitus *mundi*[4]
fugientis ut umbra;

[6] saeculi fallacis non te dementent inania spectra;
ad sibila inferni aures obtura
et eius conatus fortis infringe;

---

2   Cf. Jas, 1, 12.
3   Cf. Wis 10, 17; Sir 18, 22.
4   1Cor 7, 31.

Letter to Ermentrude of Bruges

[1] To Ermentrude, dearest sister: from Clare of Assisi the humble handmaid of Jesus Christ: health and peace. [2] I know, O dearest sister, that with the help of grace you have happily fled the mud of the world. [3] This is why I rejoice and congratulate you and rejoice all over again because with your daughters you are striding along the road of virtue.

[4] Be faithful, dearest, to the one
to whom you are promised until death.[5]
By Him you will be crowned with the laurels of life.[6]

[5] For our labour is short
but the reward eternal;
do not be confounded by the clamour of a world
as fleeting as shadows.[7]

[6] Let not the empty spectres of a deceitful world torment you.
Close your ears to the whispers of hell
And strongly resist its assaults.

---

5   1Reg 16, 20.
6   AudPov 6.
7   1LetF 12, 4; AudPov 3.

[7] adversa mala libenter sustine
et prospera bona non te extollant:
haec enim fidem exposcunt et illa exigunt;

[8] quae *Deo vovisti* fideliter *redde*[8]
et ipse retribuet.

[9] O carissima, caelum suspice
quod nos invitat,
ac tolle crucem et sequere[9] Christum
qui nos praecedit,

[10] etenim post varias et *multas tribulationes*[10]
Per ipsum intrabimus in gloriam suam.[11]

[11] Ama ex totis praecordiis Deum[12]
et *Jesum*[13] Filium eius,
pro nobis peccatoribus crucifixum,
nec de tua mente unquam excidat eius memoria;

---

8   Ps 75, 12.
9   Lk 9, 23.
10   Acts 14, 21.
11   Lk 24, 26.
12   Cf. Deut 1, 1; Lk 10, 27.
13   Cf. 1 Cor 16, 22.

[7] Freely support adversity
and be not elated when things go well
for the former challenges faith and the latter demands it.

[8] Faithfully return to God what you have promised
and He will reward you.

[9] O dearest, look to heaven
which summons us,
and take up your cross and follow Christ
who goes before us,

[10] then, after various and numerous troubles
we shall enter through Him into His glory.

[11] With your whole being, love God
and Jesus his Son,
crucified for us sinners,
never let the memory of Him slip from your mind;

[12] fac mediteris iugiter mysteria crucis,
Angoresque matris sub cruce stantis.*¹⁴*

[13] Ora et vigila*¹⁵* semper.

[14] Et *opus* quod bene coepisti instanter *consumma¹⁶*
et *ministerium* quod assumpsisti
in paupertate sancta
et humilitate sincera *adimple¹⁷*.

[15] Noli pavere, filia,
fidelis Deus in omnibus verbis suis,
et sanctus in omnibus operibus suis,*¹⁸*
effundet super te et super filias tuas
benedictionem suam;

[16] et erit auxiliator vester and consolator optimus;
redemptor noster est et merces aeterna.[19]

---

14   Cf. Jn 19, 26.
15   Cf. Mt 26, 41.
16   2 Tim 4, 5.
17   2 Tim 4, 5 and 7.
18   Ps 144, 13.
19   Cf. Gen 15, 1.

[12] always reflect on the mystery of the cross,
and the anguish of His mother,
standing firm beneath the cross.

[13] Watch and pray always.[20]

[14] The work which you have well begun,
swiftly complete,
and the ministry which you have undertaken
in holy poverty
and sincere humility,
fulfil it.

[15] Have no fear, daughter,
God is faithful in all His words
and holy in all His deeds,
He will pour out his blessing
on you and your daughters.

[16] He will be your help and the best consolation,
He is our redeemer and eternal reward.

---

20   Cf. 1Reg 22, 26.

[17] *Oremus* Deum *invicem pro* [21]nobis,
sic enim *altera alterius onus*[22] caritatis ferentes
leviter adimplebimus legem Christi.
Amen.

---

21   Jas 5, 16.
22   Gal 6, 2.

[17] Let us pray to God for each other,
then in this way we will each bear
the burdens of the other in love,
easily fulfilling the law of Christ.
Amen.

The Blessing
of Saint Clare

The Blessing of St Clare

In the highly clerical Church of the Middle Ages, it was unusual for a woman to give, let alone to write, a blessing. The exception to this would have been the Benedictine abbesses, who were women of considerable power and influence and who traditionally gave blessings to their community. The fact that Clare wrote this blessing may well be considered one of the legacies of the years she passed under the Rule of St Benedict.

The opening words echo the Blessing of Francis, also from the Book of Numbers, and we may be sure this was deliberate. However, Clare's blessing is considerably longer, more detailed and very careful to bring in both spiritual sons and daughters as well as men and women saints. At a time when the masculine pronouns habitually stood for men and women, this was an unusual emphasis.

Again we find Clare using the phrase *plantula Francisci*, the little plant of Francis, as if she sees this as one of her credentials for giving a blessing. By this phrase, she is claiming early membership of his *religio*, and then goes on to enumerate the other reasons why she is blessing the sisters – because she is their sister and mother, both to those who lived when she did and to those who will come in the future. At first, this blessing reads more like Clare's prayer for the sisters than her blessing of them but then she calls up a wonderful supporting cast to lend weight to her blessing. Her awareness of the Church Militant and the Church Triumphant is also an interesting insight into how inclusive her vision and how wide her understanding of her vocation. Her reference to the Church Triumphant recalls the angels at the top of the San Damiano Crucifix welcoming the triumphant and ascending Christ.

Manuscripts

There are three blessings of Clare, substantially the same. One is to Agnes of Prague, one to Ermentrude and one in plural form for all the sisters. The blessing to Agnes exists only in a German manuscript[1] while the others are in Flemish, French, Italian as well as Latin. The Blessing is not in the oldest known manuscript of the letters, that of Milan. The blessing for all the sisters is in a 15th century French manuscript, in the Italian Urbino manuscript and in Mark of Lisbon's *Chronicles* of 1582. The text used here is taken from the French *Ecrits* and is basically that of the Messina manuscript of the fourteenth century.

---

1   W. Seton, 'Some new sources for the life of Blessed Agnes of. Prague, including some chronological notes and a new text of the Benediction of St Clare' in *Archivum Franciscanum Historicum* 7 (1914) pp. 185-197; C. M. Borkowski, 'A Second Middle High German Translation of the Benediction of Saint Clare' in *Franciscan Studies* 36, (1976) pp. 99-104

Benedictio

[1] *In nomine Patris et Filii et Spiritus Sancti.²*

[2] *Benedicat* vobis³ *Dominus et custodiat* vos.
[3] *Ostendat faciem suam* vobis *et misereatur* vestri.
[4] *Convertat vultum suum ad* vos *et det* vobis *pacem,⁴* sororibus et filiabus meis, [5] et omnibus aliis venturis et permansuris in nostro collegio et ceteris aliis tam praesentibus quam venturis, quae finaliter perseveraverint in omnibus aliis monasteriis pauperum dominarum.⁵

[6] Ego Clara, ancilla Christi, plantula beatissimi patris nostri sancti Francisci, soror et mater vestra et aliarum sororum pauperum, licet indigna, [7] rogo Dominum nostrum Jesum Christum per misericordiam suam et intercessionem sanctissimae suae genitricis sanctae Mariae et beati Michaëlis archangeli et omnium sanctorum angelorum Dei et beati Francisci patris nostri et omnium sanctorum et sanctarum,

---

2   Cf Mt 28, 19.
3   Note the Latin plural form of 'you'; Clare is speaking to all the sisters.
4   Cf Num 6, 24-26; BLeo 1-3.
5   Cf Mt 10, 22.

Blessing

[1] In the name of the Father and of the Son and of the Holy Spirit.

[2] May the Lord bless you and keep you.
[3] May He show His face to you and be merciful to you.
[4] May He turn his face to you and give peace to you, my sisters and daughters, [5] and to all the others who will come and remain in our company,[6] and each of the others both now and to come, who will persevere to the end[7] in all the other monasteries of the Poor Ladies.

[6] I Clare, handmaid of Christ, plant of our most blessed father Saint Francis, sister and mother to you and to the other poor sisters, although I am unworthy, [7] ask our Lord Jesus Christ of His mercy, and through the intercession of His most holy mother St Mary and Blessed Michael the archangel and all the holy angels of God, and of Blessed Francis our father and of all the men and women saints,

---

6   Clare uses the word 'collegium' here, the only use of it in early Franciscan writing.
7   Cf. UltVol 1.

[8] ut ipse Pater caelestis det vobis et confirmet istam sanctissimam suam benedictionem in *caelo* et in *terra*:⁸ [9] in terra multiplicando vos in gratia et in virtutibus suis inter servos et ancillas suas in Ecclesia sua militanti; [10] et in caelo, exaltando vos et glorificando in Ecclesia triumphanti inter sanctos et sanctas suas.

[11] Benedico vos in vita mea et post mortem meam, sicut possum,⁹ de omnibus benedictionibus, [12] quibus *Pater misericordiarum*¹⁰ filiis et filiabus *benedixit* et benedicet *in caelo* et in terra, [13] et pater et mater spiritualis filiis suis et filiabus suis spiritualibus et benedixit et benedicet. Amen.

[14] Estote semper amatrices Dei, animarum vestrarum et omnium sororum vestrarum, [15] et sitis semper sollicitae observare quae Domino promisistis.

[16] Dominus *vobiscum*¹¹ sit semper et nunc vos sitis semper cum ipso. Amen.

---

8   Cf. Gen 27, 28.
9   LtErm and the Uppsala manuscript add: et plus quam pos-
     sum, 'and more than I can.' Cf. AFH 7.
10   2 Cor 1, 3; cf. Eph 1, 3.
11   Cf. 2 Cor 13, 11; cf. Jn 12, 26; cf. 1 Thess 4, 17.

[8] that the heavenly Father himself give you and confirm for you His most holy blessing, in heaven and on earth: [9] on earth, making you grow in grace and in His strength among the servants and handmaids of his Church militant; [10] in heaven raising you up and glorifying you in the Church triumphant among the men and women saints.

[11] I bless you in my life and after my death as much as I can, with all the blessings [12] with which the Father of mercies had blessed and will bless His sons and daughters in heaven and on earth, [13] and that a spiritual father and mother both have blessed and will bless spiritual sons and daughters.[12] Amen.

[14] Always be lovers of God, of your souls[13] and of all your sisters, [15] and always be careful to observe what you have promised to the Lord.[14]

[16] The Lord be with you always and now may you always be with him. Amen.

---

12   1Reg 9, 13-14; 2Reg 6, 9-10.
13   1TestF 3.
14   2TestF 4.

The Form
of Life

1253

The Form of Life

From Honorius III to Innocent IV and Approval

Beginning with the Constitutions of Hugolino (Gregory IX) of 1219, the Holy See played a prominent role in the legislation for 13th century religious women. The genius of Clare was that although she needed to incorporate papal requirements, she never lost sight of her initial call and its originality, and she remained faithful all her life to the Form of Life which Francis had given her in 1211/1212. This legislative path only came to a conclusion for her with the papal approval of her own text

For her Order, however, the papal involvement concluded later still with the publication of the Rule of Urban IV in 1263. This included Clare's Form of Life but reconciled it with the Form of Life of Hugolino and took the whole enterprise off into a far more monastic frame. The Rule of Urban was effectively imposed on all the Poor Sisters as well as on the sisters of Hugolino's Order of San Damiano in the Valley of Spoleto or Tuscany, and also embraced individual monasteries of no particular affiliation. This was a legislative tidy-up on a grand scale. One result is that the Poor Sisters of St Clare are still struggling to emerge from the legacy of Hugolino and Urban and to reveal the authentic and pure voice of Clare's Form of Life. To this day our current Constitutions show the influence of Hugolino, as Sr Diana Papa osc has shown so clearly in the work done by her community in Otranto, Italy.[1]

In addition to her personal line of development, Clare's legislation needs to be seen in this context and set beside that of the expanding Order of San Damiano which, from the time of Honorius III, had been a project dear to the Holy See. The papacy, through Cardinal Hugolino, had invested a lot of energy in organizing and legislating for the numerous groups of women who had gathered together to support each other in relatively unstructured forms of the devout life. They did not want, or for various reasons (often financial) were unable, to belong to the well-established Benedictine Order. Sometimes they were linked in one way or another with the poverty movements of the period. In the eyes of the papacy, this tended to imply two things. Either they were fervent and committed, or they were in danger of drifting off towards the heretical fringe, as so many other poverty movements had done in the recent past. This was the main reason why Honorius III sent Hugolino out to tour the communities of North Italy and to organise them, to establish them on a firm financial basis and to bring

---

1   D. Papa, <u>The Poor Sisters of St Clare</u>, translated by Sr Frances Teresa Downing, osc. Tau Publishing, Phoenix, Arizona, 2010.

them under the control of Rome. Against this backdrop, it is easy to see why Clare's independent approach was unwelcome, although there seem to have been no fears that she was linked in any way with the heretical movements. However, we should not forget that the Spoleto valley was one of the areas where the Catharist movement had considerable influence. Orthodoxy was always an issue, and we find both Francis and Clare were constantly making their allegiance to Rome very explicit and clear.

Learning from the brothers

Like Francis, Clare never ceased to look back to the text which Innocent III had approved for Francis in 1209, and to the insights which he had 'written down simply and in few words' (1TestF 15). By the time Clare was finalising her text, Francis had been dead for twenty-five years but the struggle which the friars had gone through was certainly not forgotten. The arguments and conflicts must have been for Clare in the nature of a powerful warning. Paradoxically, while Francis had such painful struggles with his brothers and it could be said that the papacy was the least of his worries, Clare had the opposite, apparently total support from her community yet she had to struggle all her life to persuade the papacy to accept the radical nature of her calling. The friars' later conflicts over their legislation and the meaning of Francis' Testament, which had all come to a head at the Chapter of 1230, meant that Clare was very much on her own in this, though it is clear from her final text that she had good advisors and a good canonist must have been among them. We can also see that she honoured Francis' Testament in the way he had wanted, not as another Rule but as "a remembrance, admonition, exhortation and [his] testament" (*Test* 34). Like Francis, she was by no means as naïve and unaware as sometimes represented.

In addition to the differing visions of their life, the brothers were also caught up in another debate which included most of the men's religious orders of the period and which went on for some centuries. This was whether the friars should or should not involve themselves with the *cura monialium*, the care of the nuns. The Friars Minor, and other friars too (e.g. Dominicans) did not want this because it left them less free to be at the service of the Church in the wider field. The papacy on the other hand wanted both. This was especially true of Hugolino and particularly after he became Gregory IX. Concerned as he was with the religious women, he saw the Friars Minor and the Dominicans as an available solution to this continuing need for someone to offer the sisters what we would now call spiritual direction as well as celebrating Mass and the sacraments with them.

This became another reason for the friars to stand back from Clare's struggle for an authentic legislation. The *cura monialium* had not been an issue for Clare while Francis lived and she had been able to choose friars to act as visitators and confessors. After his death, and as the wider debate gathered momentum, she found herself more and more constrained to accept chaplains and confessors who had no insight or understanding of her vocation and charism. Among these were Ambrose the Cistercian who had been Hugolino's chaplain, and also Bruno a secular priest as well as some Friars Minor.

By 1253, Clare's text had matured through experience and through innumerable community meetings where all major decisions were discussed and finalised. In a parallel manner, Francis' 1223 text had matured through the discussions and changes made at the Pentecost Chapters. It is clear from Clare's Rule that she knew both the 1221 and the 1223 texts well and had been living by the 1223 text for a number of years. She had gradually made a skilful adaptation of it for a group of cloistered women. We also find her incorporating some of the so-called Pre-Narbonne Constitutions of about 1239, and history shows that she carefully obeyed Francis' prohibition against seeking any letter, permission or privilege from the Roman Curia (1TestF 25) as well as his prohibition against any gloss or 'interpretation' of his text. We can also be sure that she followed, and had her own clear ideas about, the debates among the friars which lasted for some years and after her death erupted in the shape of the great discussion about *usus pauper* and *sine proprio*. It is possible, and instructive, to make a reading of Clare's Rule with reference to this developing debate about Franciscan poverty which was later to rip the friars apart. For reasons which are probably connected with those debates, Clare gathered together in Chapter Six of her Rule some of the relevant texts which she had received from Francis and did not want to be lost. These were exhortations and statements of intent and approval, all texts which validated her way of life as authentically Franciscan.

Since the early 1230s, Clare had been supported and helped by Agnes of Prague in Bohemia (1211 – 1282). Together they had struggled to be allowed to live that Form of Life which Francis had given Clare. Agnes, as sister to the King of Bohemia, spoke from a far more powerful political position. She used every advantage at her disposal, including Gregory's need of her brother, King Wenceslaus' military support, to persuade Gregory to give her that permission, but he would never agree. In fact, in a letter *Angelis gaudium* in 1238, he speaks disparagingly of the Form of Life which Francis had given to Clare, calling it *potum lactis*, milky food, baby stuff. Gregory IX did everything he could to persuade them to accept his Constitutions based on the Rule of Benedict, strongly influenced as he was by the Cistercians he loved so well but of course this would have put Clare and her sisters right outside the Franciscan family. At a later point, when Agnes had once again petitioned Innocent IV, he also replied with a very definite No and forbade her to raise the matter again (although she did).

The hard fact is that Hugolino's Constitutions were practically unliveable, so austere and almost punitive were they. As a result there was a constant flow of letters to Rome from the monasteries, all asking for dispensations, indulgences, absolutions from one or other aspect of them. This persistence was such that in the 1240s Innocent IV finally came to accept that Gregory's text was indeed impossible to live by and that it was not good to have a Rule which seemed constantly to demand sanations and absolutions. In 1247 he published a revision which, although it made no concessions to Clare about poverty, did give Francis' Rule instead of Benedict's as the fundamental text. Canonically, this change had been possible ever since the approval of Francis' Rule in 1223, which was one reason why the sisters' had felt able to continue in their persistence – canonically, they were not asking anything impossible or innovative.

While it is true that they never explicitly petitioned to follow the 1223 Rule with adaptations, and they consistently asked for Francis' Form of Life which he had given to Clare, on the other hand, both the sisters and brothers looked to the Form of Life as the foundational text which time and experience then modified. Clare was asking that her experience be recognised as equally valid with that of the brothers. Clare, as a woman, was implicitly asking for a status equal to that of the men – something which 13th century legislation and thinking could not encompass. In fact Clare seems to have believed that this Rule of 1223 was substantially the Rule by which she was already living since the sisters and friars had been one *religio* in the very beginning. However we also know that in papal documents, which is what matters, the friars, but not the sisters, were recognized as a new religious family from 1220 onwards. This meant that from that date on, they were called an *Ordo* and no longer a *religio*, so it is interesting to find Clare's Testament speaking about the *religio* of the Friars and Sisters.[2] Did Clare consider that she had in fact become an *Ordo* together with the friars? It seems likely but we do not know. We do know that in 1253, she felt able to speak of the 'Order of Poor Sisters' and to state clearly 'which the Blessed Francis founded' – two

---

2   *… cardinali, qui religioni Fratrum Minorum et nobis fuerit deputatus,'* TestCl 44.

statements which Hugolino would not have welcomed had he been alive and which the leadership of the friars was not eager to accept either.

By 1247, the stage for religious women of a Franciscan nature was very much complicated by another factor, the so-called Minoresses. These were groups of women, or even individuals, living an unstructured life, out of enclosure, rather on the lines of the friars minor with whom they claimed kinship. The papacy found them problematic and was ill at ease with women wandering around unchaperoned, which may be relevant to the frequently asked question about whether Clare wanted to live in enclosure or not. The situation of the Minoresses suggests that had she wanted to be on the road with the brothers then this would have been possible although it was most unlikely that she would ever have gained papal approval for it. As far as we know, the Minoresses had no immediate influence on or even connection with Clare but their existence may have strengthened that resolve of the papacy to gather all the women under one large papal umbrella.

This situation was finally brought to a conclusion by the personal impact of Clare herself on Innocent IV. It is worth mentioning that Clare was known personally, and was highly respected, by three popes: Gregory IX,

Innocent IV and Alexander IV. It tells us something about her character and personality, about her genius we might say, that she made such an impression on these highly intelligent men who were utterly dedicated to the welfare of the Church. In 1253, Innocent IV visited Clare on her death bed. His biographer, the friar minor Nicolò da Calvi, who had been Innocent's secretary and became his biographer as well as bishop of Assisi, tells us that Innocent went twice to San Damiano between April and August of 1253 while the Curia was in Assisi. Innocent was deeply impressed by Clare, heard her confession and agreed to approve the text of her Rule, at least for her own monastery of San Damiano. For Clare, to receive papal approval for her Form of Life which was substantially that given her by Francis 32 years before and to which she had been faithful ever since, was a powerful and emotional experience. We are told that she kissed the document over and over again, and died holding it in her hand. We are also told, in the Life of Agnes of Prague, that she sent a copy off to Agnes as soon as it was approved. This suggests that the copy had already been prepared, since the Rule is long enough to require a certain time for copying, which in turn suggests that although it was such an emotional moment for Clare, she also kept a firm grip on the political way forward for the wider promoting of her form of life. It was one which she believed with all her heart was a true following in the footsteps of the incarnate and humble Christ.

To put into effect his promise to Clare, Innocent set in motion a chain of events:

➢ 9 August 1253 - He confirmed by the letter *Solet Annuere* the approval which Cardinal Rainaldo had given to her rule the previous year. At the time, Rainaldo (later Alexander IV) was Bishop of Ostia and Velletri and Cardinal Protector of the Order, which meant both Friars Minor and Poor Ladies, a fact that suggests some legislative recognition of Clare's understanding that they were one Order.

➢ 10 August - Innocent sent a letter to Clare at San Damiano telling her this.

➢ 11 August - Clare died.

➢ 12 August - Clare's funeral took place at San Damiano, at which Innocent indicated that he wanted to celebrate a Mass for Virgins, in other words to canonise her at once. Rainaldo suggested that he follow the Canonisation Process, newly initiated by Innocent III at the IVth Lateran Council, and Innocent agreed. After the funeral her body was taken to the Church of San Giorgio within the city walls, where Francis too had rested for two years while the Basilica was being built. Clare's body was there for rather longer, until her basilica was completed and consecrated in 1263.

Later Events

➢ 1263 Urban IV wanted to gather together all the groups of religious women, including those in Hugolino's *Order of San Damiano and the Valley of Spoleto* and those who looked to Clare for leadership especially in the matter of poverty. With this end in view, he wrote and promulgated another Rule for a new Order which he called the Order of Saint Clare. This later became known as the Urbanist Rule and, because it was imposed by the papacy, it had the sad result that the original text of Clare was officially overtaken.

➢ It was not entirely forgotten however, and in 1266 Clement IV confirmed Innocent IV's *Solet Annuere* for the Monastery in Assisi which meant that the Assisi monastery could follow the Rule of Clare. This had far-reaching repercussions because it meant that Clare's text was never entirely forgotten. The reform of Perugia in the late 1400s looked back to it, and so did that of St Colette.

➢ Finally, after Vatican II, Clare's text became the official Rule of the whole Order of St Clare. Even today the ramifications of this are still being worked through along with the growing realisation that many articles in the current Constitutions of the Order are still influenced by Urban's Rule of 1263 rather than by Clare's definitive text.

The Content of the Approval

In his letter covering the long-desired approval of Clare's Rule, Innocent IV used a short phrase which sums up the way of life she had asked him to confirm. He says:

> On your part, you have made a humble request to us that we confirm, by our apostolic guarantee, the form of life which Blessed Francis gave you, according to which you are committed to living together in a spirit of unity and vowed to most high poverty…[3]

'Living together in the spirit of unity and vowed to most high poverty' – *communiter in spiritum unitate ac voto altissimae paupertatis* - this is the most succinct description we have of Clare's vision and call, the most concise description of the Poor Clare way of life.

---

3   RegInn, Introduction to the *Form of Life*.

It is worth pausing to look at Rainaldo's letter of 1252 to see how he had defined their life. Rainaldo says:

> ... that you, beloved daughters in Christ, have despised the pomps and delights of the world and, following in the footprints of Christ Himself and His most holy mother, have chosen to live enclosed in body and to serve the Lord in supreme poverty, so that you might be able to serve the Lord with a free spirit…

We do not know if Clare or Rainaldo prepared this petition. If Clare, then this is one of only two occurrences in Clare's writings of the phrase 'enclosed' in the form of 'enclosed in body' *incluso corpore*. The other time is in the opening sentences of the first letter to Agnes, where she says she is the 'useless handmaid of the enclosed ladies of the monastery of San Damiano'.[4] It is tempting but not accurate, to identify this word with 'enclosure' as we currently understand it. The word *clausura* did not come into use until after the death of Clare, around the time of the Bull *Periculoso* of 1298. It is far from clear what concept of enclosure Clare might have had. Hugolino's Constitutions define a very strict and separated form of life which is largely based on Hugolino's understanding of his spiritual task as one of keeping the sisters

---

4   1LtAg 2.

uncontaminated by the world. It was a very intense version of 'flight from the world' spirituality and there is a good deal of evidence to suggest that Clare's motivation was different. There is a strong oral tradition in Assisi, reinforced by the letters of Jacques de Vitry, Bishop of Acre, that in the early days, probably until the Lateran reforms of 1215/16, Clare and her sisters worked among the women lepers just as Francis and the brothers did among the men lepers. Given the extreme importance Francis placed on this experience, it should not surprise us to find Clare sharing it with him. From San Damiano the little chapel of La Maddalena is only about a mile down the slopes of Monte Subasio and is known to have been the chapel of the women lepers and therefore the most likely place for the sisters to have worked. Jacques de Vitry tells us that then, at nightfall, they retired to their convent for prayer.

The sources also suggest that she and her sisters most probably lived along the lines of the *eremo*, the hermitage, as many of the early brothers were doing when she and the first sisters joined in 1212-1219. Some think the Rule for those living in Hermitages was written in the light of what Francis saw the sisters doing at San Damiano, while others think the Rule came first and this was how Clare, Agnes and the others were living. In the beginning their way of life was necessarily somewhat experimental as they learned to respond to this wholly new call from God. With the passage of time they moved into the post-Lateran IV situation, and coupled with the 1220s transition from *religio* to *ordo* and the conflict that culminated in 1230 with *Quo elongati,* that fluid, experimental stage came to an end. Hugolino's work had the result of forcing Clare to articulate her vision, as well as fight for it. Her community was always a bit of an anomaly as – unlike the other communities - it was never linked juridically to Rome but remained under the jurisdiction of the Bishop of Assisi. For many years this was the same Guido who had helped both her and Francis in the beginning. This situation posed no problem until they began to expand into other dioceses. Most of the other communities belonged to the *Order of San Damiano and the Valley of* Spoleto founded by Hugolino and were swiftly brought under the direct care of Rome by Hugolino himself and, in consequence, were exempt from episcopal jurisdiction. As part of the same arrangement, Hugolino also had considerable powers to intervene in the details of the sisters' way of life while Clare retained a high degree of autonomy which she used to maintain her commitment to the Form of Life which Francis had given her. This was when she began to realise that it could only be defended by approval from the highest authority in the Church.

When we look again at the two letters, that from Rainaldo and that from Innocent IV, we see a significant shift in their definitions. Rainaldo picks up on the two elements of enclosure and poverty to identify Clare's form of life, while Innocent, perhaps moved by the charisma of Clare herself or, perhaps, quoting her words in her petition to him, says that she was asking him to approve

> … a form of life according to which you must live in common, in a spirit of unity and the vow of most high poverty.[5]

Did Clare change her petition when she approached Innocent? Or did Rainaldo write the first petition for her? Did Rainaldo, hoping to please everyone, see those words as more likely to gain approval or as a compromise solution, incorporating Clare's community into the Hugolino group while recognising her total commitment to poverty? Did Clare see the words 'enclosed in body and to serve the Lord in supreme poverty' and realise that they did not perfectly articulate what she and her sisters were trying to do? In that case, did she substitute the far more challenging words of 'live in common, in a spirit of unity and the vow of most high poverty'. Whatever the true story, Innocent

---

5   RegInn, Introduction to the *Form of Life*.

approved a life in common, in unity, in poverty, words and concepts which occur over and over again in the Form of Life. They were the major preoccupations of a great legislator, concerned to obtain the Church's approval for the developed charism which had first been entrusted to her right back in 1212 when she was a young girl of eighteen.

BULLA INNOCENTII PAPAE IV[1]

Prologus

[1] Innocentius Episcopus, servus servorum Dei.

[2] Dilectis in Christo filiabus Clarae abbatissae, aliisque sororibus monasterii Sancti Damiani Assisinatis, salutem et apostolicam benedictionem.

[3] **Solet annuere** Sedes Apostolica piis votis et honestis petentium precibus favorem benevolum impertiri. [4] Ex parte siquidem vestra nobis exstitit humiliter supplicatum, ut cum vitae formulam, iuxta quam communiter in spirituum unitate ac voto *altissimae paupertatis*[2] vivere debetis, [5] vobis a beato Francisco traditam et a vobis sponte susceptam, [6] venerabilis frater noster Ostiensis et Velletrensis episcopus duxerit approbandam, secundum quod in ipsius episcopi litteris confectis exinde plenius continetur, [7] nos id curaremus apostolico munimine roborari. [8] Devotionis igitur vestrae precibus inclinati, quod ab eodem episcopo super hoc factum est ratum habentes et gratum, illud auctoritate apostolica confirmamus et presentis scripti patrocinio communimus, [9] tenorem litterarum ipsarum de verbo ad verbum praesentibus inseri faciente, qui talis est:

---

1   Text taken from *Ecrits*, ed. Becker, Godet, Matura, Les Editions du Cerf, Paris 1985.

2   Cf 2 Cor 8,2.

The Bull of Pope Innocent IV (*Solet annuere*[a])
Prologue

[1] Innocent, Bishop, servant of the servants of God.[3]

[2] To Clare and the other sisters in the monastery of San Damiano of Assisi, beloved daughters in Christ, health and apostolic blessing.

[3] **It is the custom** for the Apostolic See[4] to grant the devout requests of those who ask, and to look on their honest petitions with kindly favour. [4] Now you, on your part, have made a humble request to us that we would take care to confirm with apostolic authority a form of life by which you would live together in a spirit of unity and with the vow of most high poverty.[5] [5] This form of life was given you by Blessed Francis and freely accepted by you;[6] [6] and our venerable brother the Bishop of Ostia and Velletri has judged it good to grant it his approval. This is fully expressed in the letter written by that same Bishop [7] and which we confirm with our apostolic authority. [8] Turning then to the desire of your devotion,[7] holding it as already ratified and agreeing with that which was done by that same Bishop,

---

3   2Reg Prol, 1-2.
4   2Reg Prol, 3; 1Reg Prol, 2-3.
5   2Reg 6, 5.
6   TestCl 33.
7   2Reg Prol, 5; TestCl 42.

[10] Raynaldus, miseratione divina Ostiensis et Velletrensis episcopus, carissimae sibi in Christo matri et filiae dominae Clarae, abbatissae Sancti Damiani Assisinatis, [11] eiusque sororibus, tam praesentibus quam futuris, salutem et benedictionem paternam.

[12] Quia vos, dilectae in Christo filiae, mundi pompas et delicias contempsistis, [13] et ipsius Christi et eius sanctissimae matris *sequentes vestigia*,[8] elegistis habitare incluso corpora, et in paupertate summa Domino deservire, ut mente libera possitis Domino famulari: [14] nos vestrum sanctum propositum in Domino commendantes, votis vestris et sanctis desideriis libenter volumus affectu paterno favorem benevolum impertiri.

[15] Eapropter vestris piis precibus inclinati, formam vitae et modum sanctae unitatis et *altissimae paupertatis*[9] quam vobis beatus pater vester sanctus Franciscus verbo et scripto tradidit observandam. [16] praesentibus annotatam, auctoritate domini papae et nostra vobis omnibus vobisque in vestro monasterio succedentibus in perpetuum confirmamus, et praesentis scripti patrocinio communimus.

[17] Quae talis est :

---

8   1 Pet 2, 21.
9   2 Cor 8,2.

we confirm it by our apostolic authority [9] and with the patronage of this present writing into which has been inserted word by word the burden of his letter. That letter is as follows:

[10] Rainaldo, by divine mercy bishop of Ostia and Velletri, to his dearest mother and daughter in Christ, the lady Clare, abbess of San Damiano of Assisi, [11] and to her sisters present and future, health and a paternal blessing.

[12] Beloved daughters in Christ, because you have despised the pomps and delights of the world, [13] following the footprints of Christ himself and his most holy mother, and have chosen to live enclosed in body and to serve the Lord in supreme poverty so that you can serve the Lord with liberty of spirit: [14] we, commending your holy *propositum*[b] in the Lord with fatherly affection, freely desire to grant your vows and your holy desires.

[15] This is why, moved by your devout prayers, we confirm in perpetuity, by the authority of the lord Pope and our own, for all you and those who will come after you in your monastery, the form of life and way of holy unity and most high poverty which your blessed father Saint Francis gave you in word and writing to observe, [16] and we have noted it in this present document. By this present writing we give you this for your observance. [17] This is the rule:

Notes to the Papal Bull

[a] *Solet annuere* 9 August 1253 is the name by which this document is known. It confirms Clare's Form of Life, but only for the monastery of San Damiano. In fact there are several bulls called *Solet annuere*, all of them granting approval of a rule or form of life. This one is dated Assisi, 9 August, 1253. Clare received it on 10 August.

The original of this Bull is in the archives of the Protomonastery in Assisi. The documents of this archive are fully described by P. Robinson ofm in *Inventarium omnium documentorum in Archivo Protomonasterii S. Clarae Assisienis nunc asservantur*, in *AFH* 1, (1908), 417 et seq.

[b] A *propositum*, or proposal, was the definition of a form of life granted to a new group. The approval of 1209 given to Francis was probably a propositum. If all went well, then the group would proceed to a more developed form of legislation. Although Clare's community had been in existence since 1212, these documents of approval give every sign of legislative caution.

A Summary of the Form of Life of Saint Clare

Note that the division into twelve chapters was done later for convenience and is not part of Clare's own work.

One – Rooting the text in Francis, Clare's relationship with the Gospel, with Francis, with the Church, with the Order, with the future

Two – How to join, advice on community meetings and formation

Three – The official prayer of the Community and the sacraments

Four – Structures of government, the elections, the abbess and council

Five – Silence, the parlour and other matters which help the contemplative life to flourish

Six – The heart of the Rule, on having no possessions, the beginning of a sustained reflection on *sine proprio*.

Seven – *Sine proprio* and work

Eight – *Sine proprio* and material need, the pastoral role of the abbess

Nine – *Sine proprio* when things go wrong and when out of the monastery, penance for wrong-doers, those who serve outside the monastery

Ten – *Sine proprio* in our own will, admonition and correction

Eleven – *Sine proprio* and independence, those who can enter the cloister and why

Twelve – The visitator, chaplain, cardinal protector, spiritual helpers of the community.

In the Latin text of the Form of Life, Clare's own words are printed in **bold**, Francis' words and the Rule of 1221 are in *italic* and the Rule of 1223 in ***bold italic.*** The rest of the text is either from Hugolino, Innocent IV or some other contemporary source.

Caput I

[1] Forma *vitae* **ordinis sororum pauperum quam beatus Franciscus instituit**[1] *haec est:*

[2] Domini nostri Ihesu Christi sanctum evangelium observare, vivendo in obedientia, sine proprio et in castitate.

[3] **Clara, indigna ancilla Christi et plantula**[a] **beatissimi patris Francisci,** *promittit obedientiam et reverentiam domino papae* **Innocentio et** *successoribus eius canonice intrantibus et ecclesiae romanae.* [4] **Et sicut in principio conversionis suae una cum sororibus suis promisit obedientiam beato Francisco ita eandem promittit inviolabiliter servare successoribus suis.** [5] *Et aliae* sorores *teneantur* **semper** *successoribus* **beati Francisci et sorori Clarae** *et* **aliis abbatissis canonicae electis** *ei succedentibus obedire.*

---

1   Text in bold: Clare; italic: 1221; italic bold: 1223.

In the name of the Lord!
The beginning of the form of life of the poor sisters

1 [1] The form of life of the Order of Poor Sisters[2] which blessed Francis instituted, is this:[b]

[2] to observe the holy Gospel of our Lord Jesus Christ,[3] living in obedience, without ownership and in chastity.

[3] Clare, the unworthy handmaid of Christ, and the little plant of the most blessed father Francis,[4] promises obedience and reverence to the Lord Pope Innocent and his canonically elected successors, and to the Roman Church. [4] And just as, at the beginning of her conversion,[5] together with her sisters, she promised obedience to blessed Francis, so in the same way she promises to keep it inviolably to his successors. [5] The other sisters shall always be bound to obey the successors[c] of blessed Francis,[6] of sister Clare and of the other canonically elected abbesses.

---

2   1Reg 1, 2.
3   2Reg 1, 1-2; 1Reg 1, 2; TestCl 17.
4   TestCl 37, 48; BlCl 6; 1Reg 1, 3.
5   TestCl 47.
6   1Reg 21, 6.

Notes to Chapter One

^a Cf 2Cel 109 where (in the Latin) Celano uses the same phrase of Bernard of Quintavalle and *LegMaior* 4, 6 where Bonaventure uses it of Clare. This suggests that the phrase may have been in common use and referred to those received into the Order by Francis himself. Cf TestCl 37.

^b Clare's Rule is based on that of Francis' approved in 1223. She stresses that Francis gave this form of life to her, that he began the Order of Poor Sisters and she bears witness that her form of life in 1253 is in direct organic continuity with that of their beginning.

^c There is a juridical as well as a spiritual link with the Friars Minor.

Caput II

[1] *Si qua divina inspiratione venerit ad* **nos** *volens vitam istam accipere* **abbatissa sororum omnium consensum requirere teneatur,** [2] **et si maior pars consenserit, habita licentia domini cardinalis protectoris nostri possit eam** *recipere.* [3] **Et si recipiendam viderit,** *diligenter examinet eam* **vel examinari faciat** *de fide catholica et ecclesiasticis sacramentis.* [4] *Et si haec omnia credat et velit ea fideliter* **confiteri** *et usque in finem firmiter observare* [5] *et* **virum** *non habet vel si habet et iam* **religionem** *intravit auctoritate diocesani episcopi, voto continentiae iam emisso, aetate* **etiam** *longaeva vel infirmitate aliqua seu fatuitate ad huius vitae observantiam* **non impediente,** [6] *diligenter exponatur ei tenor vitae nostrae.*

[7] **Et si idonea fuerit, dicatur ei** *verbum sancti evangelii, quod vadat et vendat omnia sua et ea pauperibus erogare.* [8] *Quod si facere non poterit, sufficit ei bona voluntas.*[1]

---

1   Cf. Mt 9, 21.

How postulants are to be accepted

2 [1] If anyone shall come to us by divine inspiration[a] wanting to accept this life,[2] the abbess must seek the consent of all the sisters;[b] [2] and if the majority shall have consented, and having the permission of our lord Cardinal Protector,[c] she can receive her. [3] If the abbess sees that she (the postulant) is acceptable, let her examine her carefully, or have her examined, about the catholic faith and the sacraments of the Church.[3] [4] If she believe all this[4] and wants to believe and keep it to the end, [5] if she have no husband or if she has, then he - with the authority of the diocesan bishop and after having made a vow of continence – has already entered religious life, and if there be no impediment to observing this kind of life on the grounds of advanced age or weakness,[5] [6] then she shall carefully explain the tenor of our life to her.[6]

[7] If she be receptive, let the words of the Gospel be said to her: that she go and sell all she has and seek to give it to the poor.[7] [8] If she be unable to do this, then her good will is enough.

---

2   1Reg 2, 11; 2Reg 2, 2.
3   2Reg 2, 3.
4   2Reg 2, 4-5.
5   Cf. RegHug 4.
6   1Reg 2, 3.
7   1Reg 1, 3; 2, 4; 2Reg 2, 7-8; 1TestF 19.

[9] *Et caveat* **abbatissa** *et eius* **sorores** *ne sollicitae sint de rebus suis temporalibus, ut libere faciat de rebus suis quicquid Dominus inspiraverit ei. [10] Si tamen consilium requiratur, mittant eam ad aliquos* **discretos et** *Deum timentes,[8] quorum consilio bona sua pauperibus erogentur.*
[11] ***Postea*** capillis tonsis in rotundum **et** deposito habitu saeculari, *concedat ei* **tres** tunicas et mantellum.
[12] **Deinceps extra monasterium**[d] **sine utili,** rationabili, **manifesta et probabili** causa eidem **exire** non liceat. [13] *Finito vero anno probationis, recipiatur ad obedientiam promittens vitam et* **formam paupertatis nostrae** *in perpetuum* observare. [14] **Nulla infra tempus probationis veletur.**

[15] **Mantellulas etiam possint sorores habere pro alleviatione et honestate servitii et laboris.** [16] **Abbatissa vero de vestimentis discrete eisdem provideat** *secundum* qualitates **personarum** *et loca et tempora et frigidas regiones, sicut necessitati viderit expedire.* [17] **Iuvenculae in monasterio receptae infra tempus aetatis legitimae tondeantur in rotundum et**

---

8   Cf. Acts 13, 16.

[9] Let the abbess and the sisters be careful not to concern themselves about her temporal goods[9] so that she can freely do what the Lord shall inspire her to do. [10] If she need advice, let them send her to some discreet and God-fearing people on whose advice she can distribute her goods to the poor. [11] After her hair has been tonsured[e] and she has laid aside her secular clothes, let three tunics[10] and a mantle be given her.[f] [12] After that, it will not be lawful for her to leave the monastery[11] except for a useful, reasonable, obvious and approved cause.[12] [13] Once her year of probation has finished, she shall be received to obedience, promising always to observe this life and the form of our poverty.[13] [14] During the year of probation, no-one shall wear a veil.

[15] The sisters can have small mantles[14] for warmth and if they need them for their service and work. [16] But the abbess must wisely provide them with clothes,[15] according to the quality of the person, the place, the weather and the cold in some regions, just as it shall seem to her to be necessary. [17] The very young, received

---

9   1Reg 2, 5-6; 2Reg 2, 9-10.
10   1Reg 2, 7; 2Reg 2, 11.
11   1Reg 2, 3; 2Reg 2, 13; RegCl 11, 8.
12   Cf. RegHug 4.
13   1Reg 2, 8; 2Reg 2, 12.
14   1Reg 2, 13; 2Reg 2, 15.
15   2Reg 4, 3.

depositu habitu saeculari induantur panno religioso, sicut visum fuerit abbatissae. [18] **Cum vero ad aetatem legitimam venerint, indutae iuxta formam aliarum faciant professionem suam.** [19] **Et tam ipsis quam aliis novitiis abbatissa sollicite** magistra **provideat de** discretioribus **totius monasterii,** [20] quae **in sancta conversatione et honestis moribus iuxta formam professionis nostrae** eas **diligenter** informet.

[21] **In examinatione et receptione sororum** servientium **extra monasterii** servetur **formam praedicta;** [22] **quae** *possint portare calceamenta.* [23] **Nulla nobiscum residentia faciat in monasterio, nisi recepta fuerit secundum formam professionis nostrae.** [24] **Et amore sanctissimi et dilectissimi pueri pauperculis panniculis involuti in praesepio reclinati**[16] **et sanctissimae matris eius** *moneo*, **deprecor** *et exhortor* **sorores meas ut** *vestimentis* **semper** *vilibus induantur.*

---

16   Cf. Luke 2, 7 and 12.

young, received when they are younger than the permitted age,[17] shall be tonsured and clothed in the habit of religious as the abbess shall decide. [18] Then when they reach the lawful age, they shall be clothed in the same way as the others and make their profession. [19] The abbess shall lovingly give a mistress to them and to the other novices from among the more discreet of the whole monastery [20] who shall instruct them in holy living and appropriate customs, according to the form of our profession.[18]

[21] Let the above form be observed for the examination and reception of the sisters who are to serve outside the monastery, [22] and they may wear[g] shoes.[19] [24] Nobody can reside in the monastery with us unless she has accepted the form of our profession.[20] [25] And for love of the most holy and most beloved Baby,[21] laid in a manger and wrapped in swaddling clothes, and for love of His most holy mother, I advise, I beg and I urge my sisters always to clothe themselves in poor[h] garments.[22]

---

17   Cf. RegSB 55, 1-2.
18   Cf. RegInn 1.
19   2Reg 2 16.
20   RegCl 6, 7.
21   TestCl 45; 4LtAg 19-21.
22   2Reg 2 17.

Notes to Chapter Two

a   For Clare, as for Francis, the touchstone of all vocational discernment was this, whether or not the person has been called by Divine inspiration. She accepts no other reason for being part of the community, and never changes in her attitude to the others as sisters whom the Lord had given her.

b   Cf Constitutions of the monastery of Blessed Dominic at Mont Argis: *Priorissa etiam non recipiat aliquam sine consensu totius conventus vel amplioris partis eiusdem* – The Prioress shall not receive anyone without the consent of the whole chapter or the greater part of it.

c   The Cardinal Protector was a very real presence both for the friars and for the sisters, and it was the same Cardinal for them both.

d   Note here Francis' prescription about the brothers not leaving this *religio* (1 Reg 2, 10). For Clare, the monastery is the place where the sisters' lives are conducted, for Francis it is the *religio* or Order. Clare's prescriptions here are to be seen as referring to commitment rather than to enclosure.

e   The latin says: '*capillis tonsis in rotundum*' her hair cut or tonsured in the round, implying that there might be other forms of tonsure. We know that Francis asked for the friars to have a small tonsure, presumably one which was less obvious than the large monastic tonsure. It is also important to bear in mind that the tonsure did not signify that the person had become a religious as understood today but a penitent and as such was recognised as part of the structure of the Church. When Clare pulled off her veil before her relatives, they saw that she had been tonsured, and therefore was under the jurisdiction of the Church and no longer that of civil society. It was this more than their acceptance of her dedication which forced them to withdraw. For men, the tonsure was also a prerequisite for receiving the other minor orders.

[f] Cf Cardinal Rainaldo's letter *Quoniam frequenter* which says: *Tres etiam tunicas aut plures, si necessitas exegerit* – Three tunics or more if necessity demand. On mantles, or little cloaks, he says: *mantellum unum ordinatur ac unum curtum, si volueritis pro labor* – let them be granted one mantle or a short one for work, if they wish. The 13th century Poor Clares were popularly identified by their striped cloaks, which seems to mean that they were made from scraps of material rather than cut from one large piece of cloth. Cf *The Striped Mantle of the Poor Clares: Image and Text in Italy in the Later Middle Ages* by Cordelia Warr, paper given at the International Mediaeval Congress, Leeds, 1996. That was the normal way for penitents to dress.

This letter of Rainaldo was in mitigation of Hugolino's Constitutions (called here RegHug) and was sent to some of the monasteries of Hugolino's *Ordo Sancti Damiani*. There are several versions of this letter with small variants. The one used here is that sent to the monastery in Bressanone on 6 June 1252: cf Bullarium Franciscanun II, 305.

g   The PreNarbonne Constitutions of 1239 for the friars say: *Vestimentorum vilitas attendatur in pretio pariter et colore* – let their clothes be those of the poor in material and colour. It is interesting to find Clare incorporating the ongoing directives of the friars into her own legislation. It indicates how closely she identified their two forms of life. *AFH* 83 (1990) 50-95.

h   That is, clothes which are not expensive.

Caput III

[1] Sorores litteratae *faciant divinum officium* secundum consuetudinem fratrum minorum, [2] *ex quo habere poterunt breviaria,* **legendo sine cantu.** [3] **Et quae occasione rationabili non possent aliquando legendo dicere horas suas, liceat eis sicut aliae sorores dicere pater noster.**[1] [4] Quae **vero** litteras nesciunt dicant viginti quatuor pater noster pro matutino, pro laude V, pro prima **vero**, tertia, sexta, nona, pro qualibet istarum horarum VII, pro vesperis autem XII, pro completorio VII. [5] Pro defunctis **etiam dicant in vesperis** *VII pater noster cum requiem aeternam,*[2] **pro matutino XII** [6] **cum sorores litteratae teneantur facere officium mortuorum.** [7] **Quando vero soror monasterii nostri migraverit,** *dicant* L *pater noster.*

[8] Omni tempore **sorores** ieiunent. [9] *In nativitate* **vero** *Domini,* **quocumque die venerit, bis refici possint.** [10] Cum adolescentulis, debilibus **et** servientibus **extra monasterium, sicut videbitur** abbatissae, misericorditer dispensetur.

---

1   Mt 6, 9-13.
2   Cf. 4 Esdrah 2, 34-35.

*The Divine Office, fasting,
confessions and communion*[a]

3 [1] The sisters who can read shall recite the Divine Office according to the custom[b] of the Friars Minor,[3] [2] for which reason they may have breviaries,[c] reading without chant. [3] Those who are not able to say the hours for some reasonable cause,[4] let them say the *Our Father* like the other sisters. [4] Those who do not know how to read[5] shall say twenty-four *Our Fathers*[d] for Matins; five for Lauds; seven each for Prime, Terce, Sext and None; twelve for Vespers; seven for Compline. [5] For the dead[6] they shall say seven *Our Fathers* with *Requiem eternam* and twelve for Matins [6] while the sisters who know how to read must say the Office for the Dead.[7] [7] When a sister of our monastery dies, they shall say fifty *Our Fathers*.[8]

[8] The sisters fast[9] in all seasons.[e] [9] On the Nativity of the Lord, whatever day it may fall, they may eat twice. [10] For the young, the weaker and those serving outside the monastery the abbess may, in compassion, dispense them.[f]

---

3   1Reg,3, 3-4; 2Reg 3, 2; 1TestF 22; LtOrd 52.
4   RegEr 3.
5   2Reg 3, 3-4.
6   1Reg 3, 13; 2Reg, 3, 5.
7   1Reg 3, 6.13; 2Reg, 3, 5. 6.
8   2Reg 3, 6-9.
9   1Reg 3, 15-16; 3LtAg 32-35.

[11] *Tempore vero manifestae necessitatis non teneantur* **sorores** *ieiunio corporali.*

[12] **Duodecim vicibus ad minus abbatissae licentia confiteantur in anno** [13] **et cavere debent ne alia verba** tunc **inserant, nisi** quae ad confessionem **et salutem** pertinent **animarum.**

[14] **Septem vicibus communicent, videlicet in nativitate Domini, in quinta feria maioris ebdomadae, in resurrectione Domini, in pentecoste, in assumptione beatae Virginis, in festo sancti Francisci et in festo omnium sanctorum.** [15] **Pro communicandis sanis sororibus vel infirmis capellano intus liceat celebrare.**

[11] In times of obvious need the sisters are not bound to bodily fasts.[10]

[12] Twelve times a year at least they may confess with the abbess' permission.[11] [13] Let them be careful lest any other words creep in which are not to do with their confession and the salvation of souls.

[14] Let them communicate seven times a year[12] namely: the Nativity of the Lord, Thursday in Holy Week, the Resurrection of the Lord, Pentecost, the Assumption of the Virgin, on the feast of St Francis and on the feast of All Saints. [15] In order that both the healthy and the sick sisters may communicate, the chaplain is allowed to celebrate inside the monastery.[13]

---

10   1Reg 9 20; 2Reg 3, 10.
11   1Reg 20 1-3; 2 LtF 22.
12   1Reg 20 7; 2 LtF 22.
13   RegCl 12, 10.

Notes to Chapter Three

[a] In this chapter, Clare deals with the sisters' relationship with God and the Church, in Chapter 4 their relationships with each other while Chapter 5 addresses their relationship with the rest of the world, all within the context of exploring *sine proprio* and how it is to be lived in various circumstances.

[b] The 'breviary' was the short version of the monastic office as said by the members of the Curia and travelling bishops. This was also the practice in the Rule of Innocent IV and in some other houses of other orders at the time, for instance the monastery of Blessed Dominic at Mont Argis. It was a major departure from the monastic office as celebrated in most monasteries. Innocent IV said: *secundum consuetudinem Ordinis Fratrum Minorum,* 'according to the custom of the Friars Minor'. Interestingly, when the Church's liturgy needed reform, it was to that of the friars minor that liturgists looked for restoration. Cf. *The Origins of the Modern Roman Liturgy.*

Clare's option for the friars' breviary must have meant that the sisters spent far less time in choir than was usual in monasteries of that period. For the friars, this enabled them to have time for pastoral work among the people and for contemplative time with God. Presumably Clare saw both these as having a place, time for those who came to the monastery seeking help and contemplative time with God which was personal and perhaps alone, rather than in choir and in common. Sister Benvenuta, for instance, speaks of 'the place where the Lady Clare usually went to pray' (ProcCan II, 17).

The much-discussed prohibition against chant may have arisen from the same concern that time for personal communication with God be not cut short. It should also be borne in mind that many monastic choirs of the period were highly professional in their complexity and skill; this is the century of some of the great Masses to be found today in the Graduale, and Clare perhaps wanted the Office to be such that all could take part as equals. It is hard to imagine one as in tune with Francis as Clare was, being hostile to singing and beauty. It is also important to notice that the text reads as if the phrase 'without chant' follows from 'the custom of the friars minor'. Grammatically, the Latin phrase *ex quo* governs both having breviaries and not chanting, linking both to the custom of the friars.

c This was a major investment since a breviary at that time – which had to be hand written – could cost as much as a good horse or a year's wages for an agricultural worker (Fr Thaddée Matura ofm, in a talk on the Rule).

^d Cf. Cardinal Rainaldo's letter *Quoniam frequenter: ...
et quamdiu sorores aliquae pro utilitate monasterii fuerint
extra claustrum, liceat eis cordas et caputia portare et pro
horis suis dicere Pater noster* - whenever the sisters are
out of the cloister on business of the monastery, they
may have strings of beads and for the hours can say
Our Father, 6 June 1252 version.

^e *Omni tempore* – this means in all liturgical seasons
rather than 'at all times'. Clare then subtracts Christmas
and Easter which probably meant the octave of Easter
rather than the whole time until Whitsun, but in her 3rd
letter to Agnes of Prague she expands this (3LtAg 29-
41). Cf. RegHug 7, which said: *omni tempore ieiunent
quotidie* – they shall fast daily at all seasons – including
the season of Easter and that of Christmas. Fasting is
almost the only issue on which Clare was stricter than
Francis who took a very wide view, especially for his
time. We know that he objected to Clare's own fasting
and with the help of the Bishop, took steps to limit it.

^f Cf. RegHug 7: *Hanc autem ieiunii et abstinentiae legem
adolescentulae vel anus et omnino corpore imbecilles ac
debiles omnino corpore observare minimae permittantur,
sed secundum earum imbecillitatem tam in cibariis quam
ieiuniis cum eis misericorditer dispensetur* – This law of
fasting and abstinence should not be allowed to the
young, the very old, the weak or incapable, but they

should be treated with compassion with regard to food in view of their weakness.

Hugolino's approach is stricter than that of his successor as Protector, Rainaldo who says in *Quoniam frequenter*: *Preterea servientes vestrae ... cum nimis laborant vel vadunt de loco ad locum, praeterquam in ieiuniis ab ecclesia constituis, non teneantur nisi sexta feria ieiunare* – concerning your servants, those whose work is hard or who go from place to place, except for the fasts of the church and Fridays, they are not obliged to fast.

Caput IV

[1] In electione abbatissae teneantur sorores formam canonicam observare. [2] Procurent autem ipsae festinanter habere generalem ministrum vel provincialem ordinis fratrum minorum [3] qui verbo Dei eas informet ad omnimodam concordiam et communem utilitatem in electione facienda. [4] Et nulla eligatur nisi professa. [5] Et si non professa eligeretur vel aliter daretur, non ei obediatur nisi primo profiteatur formam paupertatis nostrae. [6] *Qua decedente electio* alterius abbatissae *fiat*.

[7] Et si aliquo tempore appareret universitati **sororum** *praedictam non esse sufficientem ad servitium et communem utilitatem* **ipsarum,** *teneantur praedictae* **sorores iuxta formam praedictam** quam citius possunt *aliam sibi* **in abbatissam et matrem** *eligere*.

[8] **Electa vero cogitet quale onus in se suscepit et cui redditura est rationem**[1] **de grege sibi commisso. [9] Studeat etiam magis aliis praeesse virtutibus et**

---

1   Cf. Mt. 12, 36; Heb. 13, 17; cf. RegSB 64, 7.

The election and office of the abbess,
the chapter, the officials and the discreets

4 [1] The sisters must observe the canonical form for the election of the abbess. [2] In good time, they shall have the Minister General or a provincial of the Order of Friars Minor,[a] [3] who will instruct them in the Word of God so that the elections may be made with harmony between them and for the common good. [4] No-one is to be elected who is not professed. [5] If a non-professed be elected, or otherwise given them, they are not to obey her until she shall first have professed the form of our poverty. [6] At her death, there shall be the election of another abbess.[2]

[7] If at a given moment it seems to the sisters in general that the aforesaid abbess is not adequate for the service and common good of them all,[3] the aforesaid sisters are bound, as soon as possible, to elect another abbess and mother for themselves according to the aforesaid form.

[8] Let the one who is elected reflect on the burden she has taken on herself[b] and to whom she *must render an account*[4] of the flock committed to her.[5] [9] Let her

---

2   2Reg, 8, 3.
3   2Reg, 8, 4,5.
4   LtElias, 3-6; TestCl. 69.
5   1Reg, 4, 6; 16, 5.

sanctis moribus quam officio, ut eius exemplo provocatae sorores potius ex amore ei obediant quam timore. [10] Privatis amoribus careat, ne dum in parte plus diligit, in totum scandalum generet. [11] Consoletur afflictas, [12] sit **etiam** ultimum refugium tribulatis,[6] ne si apud eam remedia defuerint sanitatum desperationis morbus praevaleat in infirmis.

[13] **Communitatem servet in omnibus, praecipue autem in ecclesia, dormitorio, refectorio, infirmaria et vestimentis, [14] quo etiam simili modo servare eius vicaria** teneatur.

[15] *Semel* **in ebdomada ad minus abbatissa sorores sua teneatur** *ad capitulum convocare* [16] **ubi tam ipsa quam sorores de communibus et publicis offensis et negligentiis humiliter debeant confiteri. [17] Et quae tractanda sunt pro utilitate et honestate monasterii ibidem conferat cum omnibus sororibus suis. [18] Saepe enim Dominus quod melius est iuniori revelat.**

---

6   Cf Ps. 31, 7.

study to go before them by virtue and holy behaviour rather than by reason of her office, so that moved by her example, the sisters may obey her through love rather than fear.ᶜ [10] Let her beware of favourites,ᵈ lest giving more love to the part cause scandal to the whole.⁷ [11] Let her console those who are afflicted. [12] Let those who are troubled have to seek no further for a refuge, for those who are less strong may be overcome by the illness of despair if they do not find a health-giving remedy with her.⁸

[13] Let her observe the communityᵉ life in every way, but especially in the church, the dormitory, the refectory,ᶠ the infirmary and in clothing, [14] and the vicaressᵍ shall be obliged to do the same.

[15] At least once a week the abbess must call the sisters together in chapter.⁹ [16] There she, as well as the sisters, must humbly confess their common and public offences and negligences. [17] Let her confer with all her sisters about whatever is for the good and integrity of the monastery,¹⁰ [18] for the Lord often reveals to a youngerʰ what is best.¹¹

---

7   TestCl 61-62; 1Reg 7, 2 ; 2Cel 185.
8   TestCl 38, 63; cf 2Cel 185.
9   2Reg 8, 6.
10   Cf. 1LtAg 3.
11   Cf. RegSB 3,3.

[19] **Nullum debitum grave fiat, nisi de communi consensu sororum et manifesta necessitate et hoc per** procuratorem. [20] **Caveat autem abbatissa cum sororibus suis, ne aliquod** depositum **recipiatur in monasterio,** [21] **Saepe enim de huiusmodi turbationes et** *scandala oriuntur.*

[22] **Ad conservandam** unitatem mutuae **dilectionis et pacis, de communi consensu omnium sororum omnes** officiales **monasterii eligantur,** [23] **et eodem modo octo ad minus sorores de** discretioribus **eligantur, quarum in hiis quae forma vitae nostrae requirit, abbatissa uti consilio semper teneatur.** [24] **Possint etiam sorores et debeant, si eis utile et expediens videatur, officiales et discretas aliquando removere et alias loco ipsarum eligere.**

[19] No heavy debt shall be undertaken without the common consent of the sisters[i] and an obvious necessity, and they shall do this through a procurator.[j] [20] Let the abbess and her sisters take care not to receive any deposits into the monastery[k] [21] because trouble and scandal often arise from this.[l]

[22] In order to conserve the unity of mutual love and peace,[12] the officials of the monastery shall be elected[13] by the common consent of all the sisters. [23] In the same way, at least eight sisters from among the more discreet shall be elected so that the abbess can make use of their counsel[m] in those things which the form of our life demands. [24] The sisters can, and if it seem useful and expedient to them they must, remove any of the officials and discreets and elect others in their place.

---

12   RegCl 10, 7; TestCl 59, 69.
13   RegCl 11, 4.

Notes to Chapter Four

a   This goes back to the Rule of Innocent IV who required the general or provincial to be present in order to confirm the election. Note that Clare defines no official role for the friars beyond that of encouraging the sisters beforehand to harmony and the common good. For Clare, the election is valid by reason of the community's' vote, not by reason of the general or provincial's approval.

b   Cf. RegSB 64, 7-8: *Ordinatus autem abba cogitet semper quale onus suscepit et cui redditurus est rationem villicationis suae, sciatque sibi oportere prodesse magis quam praeesse* – Once elected, let the abbot always consider the burden which he has taken upon himself and to whom he must render an account of his stewardship, and let him know that he should serve rather than be at the head.

c   Cf. RegSB: *Et studeat plus amari quam timeri* – let him study to be loved rather than feared. Augustine also speaks about example and a leadership of love: *plus a vobis amari adpetat quam timeri, semper cogitans Deo se pro vobis redditurum esse rationem* – that they may follow you for love rather than fear, always being conscious of the one to whom you render an account. *Regula tertia vel Praeceptum* VII, 3.

^d Cf. 2Cel 185 speaking of the Minister General: *Homo qui privatis amoribus careat, ne dum in parte plus diligit, in toto scandalum generat. [...] Homo qui consoletur afflictos cum sit ultimum refugium tribulatis, ne si apud eum remedia defuerint sanitatum, desperationis morbus praevaleat in infirmis -* A man without favourites (particular loves) fearing lest cherishing one, he generate scandal in all. [...] A man who consoles the afflicted, being the last refuge for those in trouble, fearing lest with him they find no remedy, the sickness of despair overcome them.

^e This is the only time Clare uses the word *communitas* and almost the only time it turns up in any early Franciscan document.

^f Cf. Constitutions of the monastery of Blessed Dominic at Mont Argis: *Priorissa comedat in refectorio et cybariis conventus sit contenta. […] Si autem priorissa infirmari contigerit, in infirmaria cum aliis procuratur –* The prioress shall eat in the refectory and be content with convent food. [...] If the prioress fall ill, she shall be in the infirmary with the others.

^g This seems to be an office unique to the Franciscan family. In 1215 Clare was obliged to accept the title of abbess but with the office of vicaress she is in line with Francis' own practice of appointing a vicar to govern in his absence.

^h For many years this was thought to read *minori* not *iuniori*, the lesser instead of the younger, but the recent critical edition of the Rule has reverted to an exact quotation from Benedict. It seems that when the original manuscript of Innocent IV (in the archives of the Protomonastery) was checked, there was found to be a hole in that particular place. The reading of *iuniori* was preferred by the editors because there is no manuscript giving *minori* earlier than 15th century. *Cf. Saepe enim Dominus quod melius est minori revelat: A five-hundred year-old erroneous reading* by Sr Chiara Agnese Acquadro osc, *Collectanea Franciscana* 71 (2001).

ⁱ Clare seems to have been aware of the Constitutions of other Orders of the period, eg Trinitarians, who also made decisions in common and at a weekly chapter. Cf. *Sinossi cromatica* p. 19.

^j The procurator was another requirement of Innocent's Rule and echoes his arrangement for the friars in *Ordinem vestrum* (14 November 1245) and *Quantum studiosus* (19 August 1247).

^k This refers to the practice of that time of using the monasteries as a bank where jewels and even money could be deposited. Banking, as we know it, was only just beginning and had yet to take over major financial practices from the monasteries. Until then, stability in society was largely rooted in monastic life.

[1]   This is another departure from the monastic practice in which the governing body was the abbess and council. With Clare it was, and is, the abbess and sisters formally assembled in chapter.

[m]   PreNarbonne Constitutions 6: *cum fratrum loci consilio discretorum* – discreet counsellors from the local brethren; Pre-Narbonne 9: *teneatur custos illius custodiae de discretorum aliquorum consilio* – the guardian must himself be supported by the advice of some discreet brothers.

Caput V

[1] **Ab hora** completorii **usque ad** tertiam **sorores** silentium teneant, exceptis **servientibus extra monasterium.** [2] Sileat etiam **continue** in ecclesia, dormitorio, in refectorio **tantum** dum comedunt, [3] **praeter quam** in infirmaria, **in qua pro recreatione et** servitio infirmarum loqui **discrete semper sororibus liceat.** [4] **Possint** tamen semper et ubique breviter submissa voce quod necesse **fuerit insinuare.**

[5] **Non liceat** sororibus loqui ad locutorium **vel ad cratem sine licentia** abbatissae **vel eius vicariae.** [6] **Et licentiatae ad locutorium loqui non audeant, nisi praesentibus et** audientibus duabus **sororibus.** [7] **Ad** cratem **vero accedere non praesumant, nisi praesentibus tribus ad minus per abbatissam vel eius vicaria assignatis de illis octo discretis, quae sunt electae ab omnibus sororibus pro consilio abbatissae.** [8] Hanc **formam** loquendi **teneantur pro se** abbatissa **et eius vicaria observare.**

Silence, the parlour, the grille

5 [1] From the hour of Compline until Terce the sisters shall keep silence,[1] except those who serve outside the monastery.[a] [2] Let silence normally be kept in the church, in the dormitory and in the refectory while they are eating,[b] [3] but not in the infirmary where the sisters can always speak for the recreation and care of the sick sisters.[2] [4] However wherever the sisters are they can always[c] say what is necessary, quietly and briefly.[d]

[5] The sisters may not speak in the parlour or at the grille without permission of the abbess or her vicaress, [6] and those who do have permission should not speak except in the presence and hearing of two sisters. [7] Nor should they presume to speak at the grille[3] except in the presence of at least three assigned by the abbess or her vicaress from the eight discreets elected by all the sisters to advise the abbess. [8] This form of speaking must also be observed for herself by the abbess[e] and her vicaress.[4]

---

1   1Reg 11, 1; RegErem. 5, 7; cf. RegInn 3.
2   3LtAg 31.
3   RegCl 8, 20.
4   RegCl 8, 21.

[9] **Et hoc de** crate rarissime, **ad portam vero nullatenus** fiat. [10] Ad quam cratem pannus interius apponatur, **qui non removeatur nisi cum proponitur verbum Dei vel aliqua alicui loqueretur.** [11] Habeat **etiam** hostium ligneum **duabus diversis** seris ferreis, **valvis et vectibus optime communitum,** [12] **ut in nocte maxime duabus** clavibus **obseretur, quarum unam habeat abbatissa, aliam vero sacrista;** [13] **et** maneat semper **obseratum,** nisi cum auditur divinum officium **et** pro causis superius memoratis.

[14] **Nulla ante solis ortum vel post solis occasum loqui ad createm alicui ullatenus debeat.** [15] **Ad** locutorium vero **semper** pannus **qui non removeatur** interius **maneat.** [16] **In quadragesima sancti Martini et quadragesima maiori nulla loquatur ad locutorium,** [17] **nisi sacerdoti causa confessionis vel alterius manifestae necessitatis, quod reservetur in prudentia abbatissae vel eius vicariae.**

[9] Speaking at the grille should happen very rarely and at the door, never.[f] [10] Let there be a curtain on the inside of the grille which is only drawn back during some spiritual conference or when a sister is speaking to someone. [11] Let the wooden door have two separate iron locks with bolts and bars in good condition[5] [12] so that, especially at night, it can be locked with two keys of which the abbess has one and the sacristan the other. [13] Let it always be kept closed except when hearing the divine office and for the reasons given above.

[14] Nobody may speak in the parlour before sunrise or after sunset.[6] [15] In the parlour there shall always be a curtain across the inside [of the grille] which must not be drawn back. [16] During the Lent of St Martin and during the great Lent, let nobody speak in the parlour [17] except with a priest for confessions or for some other obvious necessity, which depends on the prudence of the abbess or her vicaress.[7]

---

5   RegCl 11, 3-5.
6   RegCl 11, 8.
7   RegCl 3, 13.

Notes to Chapter Five

[a] PreNarbonne Constitutions 51: *Silentium a dicto completorio usque ad pretiosam servetur* – Let silence be kept from compline until breakfast.

[b] Cf. Rule of the Order of the Most Holy Trinity: *Silentium observet semper in ecclesia sua, semper in refectorio, semper in dormitorio* – Let silence always be kept in their church, always in the refectory, always in the dormitory.

PreNarbonne Constitutions 52: *Sileatur etiam in claustro, choro, studio, dormitorio et refectorio dum comeditur* – Let it (silence) be kept in the cloister, choir, dormitory, and refectory while there is eating.

[c] Cf. RegHug 6.

[d] Cf. Rule of Venerable Stephen Muratensis 47: *Aliud autem silentium genus quod est tacere inutilia et loqui necessaria, a singulis fratribus semper et ubique et submissa voce significare quod necesse est* – There is another kind of silence which is to be silent about non-essentials and to speak what is necessary, to signify what is necessary to each of the brothers always and everywhere.

PreNarbonne Constitutions 53: - *liceat tamen breviter et submissa voce significare quod necesse est* – It is always lawful to say what is necessary briefly and quietly.

[e] Cf. RegHug 6.

^f It is worth comparing this chapter with Chapters 6 and 11 of Hugolino's Rule and Chapter 9 of Innocent's Rule to see the background against which Clare was writing. She is dealing here with the 'how' of silence, practical arrangements for silence and for speech. There seem to have been, at San Damiano, three points of communication with the outside world, the main door (the one which fell off its hinges), the parlour and the grille (ProcCan V, 5).

Caput VI

[1] Postquam altissimus Pater caelestis per gratiam suam cor meum dignatus est illustrare, ut exemplo et doctrina beatissimi patris nostri sancti Francisci poenitentiam facerem paulo post conversionem ipsius una cum sororibus meis obedientiam voluntarie sibi promisi.

[2] Attendens autem beatus pater quod nullam paupertatem, laborem, tribulationem, vilitatem et contemptum saeculi timeremus, immo pro magnis deliciis haberemus, pietate motus scripsit nobis formam vivendi in hunc modum:

[3] *Quia divina inspiratione fecistis vos filias et ancillas altissimi summi Regis Patris caelestis et Spiritui sancto vos desponsastis eligendo vivere secundum perfectionem sancti evangelii,* [4] *volo et promitto per me et fratres meos sempter habere de vobis tanquam de ipsis curam diligentem et sollicitudinem specialem.*

*The promise of blessed Francis
and the refusal to have possessions*[a]

6 [1] After the most high heavenly Father chose to enlighten my heart with His grace,[1] and so that I should do penance according to the example and teaching of our most blessed father Saint Francis,[2] a little while after his conversion I with my sisters freely promised[b] him obedience.[3]

[2] The blessed father, aware that we feared no poverty,[4] labour, trouble, powerlessness or the scorn of the world but rather that we held them as great delights, moved with tenderness[c] for us, wrote us this form of life:[5]

> [3] Because, by divine inspiration,[6] you have made yourselves daughters and handmaids of the most high King, the heavenly Father, and have espoused yourselves to the Holy Spirit, choosing to live according to the perfection of the holy Gospel,[7]
> [4] I want and I promise, for myself and for my brothers, always to have the same loving care and special solicitude for you as for them.[d]

---

1   TestCl 24-25, 46.
2   1TestF 1.
3   RegCl 1, 4; 1Reg 12, 3.
4   TestCl 27-28, 34; 3LtAg 38-39.
5   Cf. 2Cel 204, 5.
6   1LtF 10, 7; TestCl 34, 4Ag 4.
7   1TestF 29, 49.

[5] **Quod dum vixit diligenter implevit et a fratribus voluit semper implendum.**

[6] **Et ut nusquam declinaremus a** *sanctissima paupertate* **quam cepimus nec etiam quae post nos venturae essent, paulo ante obitum suum iterum scripsit nobis ultimam voluntatem suam dicens:**

> [7] *ego frater Franciscus parvulus volo sequi vitam et paupertatem altissimi Domini nostri Ihesu Christi et eius sanctissimae Matris et perseverare in eam usque in finem.*[8] [8] *Et rogo vos dominas meas et consilium do vobis, ut in ista sanctissima vita et paupertate semper vivatis.* [9] *Et custodite vos multum ne doctrina vel consilio alicuius ab ipsa in perpetuum ullatenus recedatis.*

[10] **Et sicut ego semper sollicita fui una cum sororibus meis sanctam paupertatem quam Domino Deo et beato Francisco promisimus custodire,** [11] **sic teneantur abbatissae quae in officio michi succedent et omnes sorores usque in finem inviolabiliter observare,** [12] **videlicet in non** *recipiendo* **vel habendo possessionem vel**

---

8   Cf. Mt. 10, 22.

[5] While he lived he carefully fulfilled this and he wanted the brothers always to fulfil it.⁹

[6] And so that neither we nor the sisters who are to come after us should ever fall away from the most high poverty^c which we have undertaken, just before his death he again wrote us his last wish. He said:

> [7] I, little brother Francis,¹⁰ want to follow the life and most high poverty of our Lord Jesus Christ and his most holy mother, and to persevere in it until the end. [8] And I ask you,^f my ladies, and give you advice that you always live in this most holy life and poverty.¹¹ [9] And take great care not to distance yourselves from this in any way through the teaching or recommendation of anyone.¹²

[10] And just as I and my sisters have always been careful to cherish the holy poverty which we have promised the Lord God and blessed Francis,¹³ [11] so shall the abbesses who will succeed me in office, and all

---

9   Cf. 2Cel 204, 6.
10   UltVol 1; RegCl 12, 13; TestCl 34, 46.
11   UltVol 2.
12   UltVol 3; 2LtAg 17-18.
13   TestCl 40, 42.

proprietatem *per se neque per interpositam personam,* [13] seu etiam aliquid quod rationabiliter proprietas dici possit, [14] nisi quantum terrae pro honestate et remotione monasterii necessitas requirit; [15] et illa terra non laboretur, nisi pro orto ad necessitatem ipsarum.

the sisters, be committed to observe it inviolably until the end. [12] They do this by neither receiving nor having possessions or ownership,[14] either personally or through another,[g] [13] nor even anything which could reasonably be called property [14] except the amount of land which is necessary for the integrity[h] and withdrawal of the monastery.[15] [15] Let this land not be worked, apart from a vegetable garden for the needs of the sisters themselves.

---

14   RegCl 8, 1; 2Reg 4, 2; 6, 2; TestCl 53-55.
15   TestCl 54-55.

Notes to Chapter Six

[a] Chapters 6 - 8 open up to us the heart of Clare's idealism and vision. They also show us how profoundly her call ran parallel to that of Francis. In Ch. 6 she sets out precious texts which she did not want to be lost, in Ch. 7 she speaks about the grace of work and specifically the grace of working with our hands, manual work, which she, like Francis, saw as integral to being poor and, especially in that culture, to being powerless, one of the *viles* who were dependent on others. However, Francis did come to recognise that intellectual work, such as that of Anthony, was also labour! Ch. 8 returns to the theme of poverty and non-ownership. It also describes the consequent place of begging, being truly a poor pilgrim dependent on others. Finally she speaks about how these values are to be dealt with when one is ill – something she knew all about. Poverty necessarily includes work, almsgiving and service of others. Clare had a clear realisation that God had entrusted a particular charism to her, that is, a service to be accomplished within the Church.

[b] In the culture of the time, to promise obedience meant to join the group. As far as we know Clare made no other profession although Gregory IX told Agnes of Prague that Clare and her sisters 'solemnly professed that Rule which was composed with careful zeal and

accepted by St Francis and afterwards confirmed by the same Pope Honorius' which could mean the *Regula Bullata* of 1223 (*Angelis gaudium,* BF I, 242).

c The Latin *pietas* has no English equivalent except to say that 'piety' is not it. The *Ecrits* translate it by *pitié* for which the English 'pity' is not a translation either! Perhaps kindness, tenderness, affection, compassion are all component parts of *pietas.*

d Surely Clare inserted this passage to stress that for Francis and herself, the brothers and sisters both responded to the one call of the same Spirit.

e For Clare, it is poverty which makes us God's *mansio,* his mansion, cf. John 14, 23 and *Sacrum Commercium* 1.

f Note the courtesy of Francis towards them and also his unfailing respect for each individual's own particular call from God. We see something parallel in the way Clare respects Agnes' articulation of the Form of Life in Prague.

g This is in direct contradiction to Innocent who said they may have both: *liceat vobis in communi redditus et possessiones recipere et habere as ea libere retinere* – you may be permitted to receive, to have in common and freely to retain produce and possessions (RegInn 11*).* Produce here implies the ability to profit by the land.

h The Latin word here is *honestas* which again has no exact English equivalent, and Clare uses it several times in different contexts. Its meaning becomes clearer when we remember that the opposite of *honestas* is *illicitas*, illicit, unlawful, and not (as we might expect) dishonest. It is not only a moral term but one which includes concepts like appropriate and even integral. For this reason it is sometimes translated here by 'integrity' but not always.

Caput VII

[1] Sorores *quibus dedit Dominus gratiam*[a] *laborandi* **post horam tertiae** *laborent* et de laboritio quod pertinet ad honestatem[b] et **communem** utilitatem, *fideliter ac devote,* [2] *ita quod excluso otio animae inimico sanctae orationis et devotionis spiritum non extinguant, cui debent cetera temporalia deservire.*

[3] **Et id quod** manibus suis **operantur** assignare in capitulo abbatissa vel eius vicaria coram omnibus teneatur. [4] **Idem fiat si aliqua elemosina pro sororum necessitatibus ab aliquibus mitteretur ut in communi pro eisdem recommendatio fiat. [5] Et haec omnia pro communi utilitate distribuantur per abbatissam vel eius vicariam de consilio discretarum.**

On the manner of working

7 [1] The sisters, to whom the Lord has given the grace of working,[1] shall work faithfully and lovingly from the hour of Terce, at work which contributes to the whole and for the common good. [2] Let them work in a way which is far from laziness, that enemy of the soul, so that they do not quench the spirit of prayer[2] which every temporal thing should serve.[c]

[3] The work of their hands shall be assigned to the sisters[d] by the abbess or her vicaress before everyone in chapter.[3] [4] They must do the same when an alms is sent by anyone for the needs of the sisters in order that recommendation may be made by all.[e] [5] And all these things must be distributed by the abbess or her vicaress for the service of all, on the advice of the discreets.

---

1   1Reg 7, 4; 2Reg 5, 2-3; 1TestF 24-25.
2   1Reg 7, 11-13; LtAnt 3.
3   2Reg 5, 4.

Notes to Chapter Seven

[a] For Francis and Clare, work is a grace and part of the fulfilment of their vocation as poor people; their order is an order of work. There is a close connection between poverty and hard, often unrewarding, work. Francis (and Clare follows him) also put a high value on manual work, working with the hands, and it was a big step for him to recognise Anthony's intellectual labour as work too. For Clare, work is an important contribution to the common life. Francis spoke critically of Brother Fly who took without giving (*Assisi Compilation* 62).

It is worth noting that the Latin *labor* means manual work, while *opus* is better translated by activity. Clare uses *labor* without any ambiguity and we know that even while she was ill, she worked at her spinning. (ProcCan I, 11) Is this another indication of her incarnational thinking, her commitment to the One of whom the Psalmist said: The heavens are the work of your hands? (Ps. 102, 25)

[b] In his Testament, Francis says: *et omnes alii fratres firmiter volo quod laborent de laboritio quod pertinet ad honestatem [...] et ego manibus meis laborabam, et volo laborare. (1 TestF 20)*

^c Jacques de Vitry records that the sisters lived from the work of their hands. (*Letter from Genoa*, October 1216*)*

^d The assigning of work is placed at chapter to keep it within the context of obedience and the common life. This also implies an acceptance that work for the sisters is their form of sharing in the wider work of God in creation and in human hearts, as well as participating in the obedient work of the Word made flesh.

^e By recommendation here, Clare means that although the gift may be sent to one sister, the response of prayer is made by all, as part of their shared life in community. This is another example of the high standard of generosity and non-acquisitiveness which she takes for granted in her sisters.

Caput VIII

[1] **Sorores** *nichil sibi approprient nec domum nec locum nec aliquam rem* [2] *et tanquam peregrinae et advenae in hoc saeculo in paupertate et humilitate Domino famulantes* **mittant** *pro elemosina confidenter,* [3] *nec oportet eas verecundari, quia Dominus pro nobis se fecit pauperem in hoc mundo.* [4] *Haec est illa celsitudo altissimae paupertatis quae vos karissimas* **sorores** *meas heredes et reginas regni caelorum instituit, pauperes rebus fecit, virtutibus sublimavit.* [5] *Haec sit portio vestra quae perducit in terram viventium.* [6] *Cui, dilectissimae* **sorores***, totaliter inhaerentes nichil aliud pro nomine Domini nostri Ihesu Christi* **et eius sanctissimae Matris** *in perpetuum sub caelo habere velitis.*

[7] **Non liceat alicui sorori litteras mittere vel aliquid recipere aut extra monasterium dare sine licentia abbatissae,** [8] nec quicquam liceat habere quod abbatissa non dederit aut permiserit.

*The sisters shall make nothing their own; on seeking alms;
on seeking alms; the sick sisters*

8 [1] The sisters shall make nothing[a] their own, neither the house nor the place nor anything at all;[1] [2] and, serving the Lord in poverty and humility, let them send for alms with confidence like pilgrims and strangers in this world,[b] [3] And they should not feel ashamed because the Lord made himself poor in this world for us.[2] [4] This is that pinnacle of most high poverty which has made you, my dearest sisters, heiresses and queens in the kingdom of heaven,[3] and which has made you poor in things but excelling in virtue. [5] Let this be your portion which leads to the land of the living. [6] Hold fast to this, most beloved sisters, and desire to have nothing else for ever in the name of our Lord Jesus Christ and his most holy mother.

[7] It shall not be permitted to any sister to send letters[c] or to receive anything or to give anything away outside the monastery without the permission of the abbess. [8] Nor shall it be permitted them to hold on to anything which the abbess has not given them or permitted.[4]

---

1   RegCl 6, 12-13; 1Reg 7, 14; 2Reg 6, 2-7; 1TestF 28-29; TestCl 52.
2   2Reg 6, 5; 1LtAg 30; 2LtAg 23.
3   AudPov 6.
4   Cf. RegSB 54.2.

[9] **Quod si a parentibus suis vel ab aliis ei aliquid mitteretur, abbatissa faciat illi dari.** [10] **Ipsa autem si indiget uti possit, sin autem sorori indigenti caritative communicet.** [11] **Si vero ei aliqua pecunia transmissa fuerit, abbatissa de consilio discretarum in hiis quae indiget illi faciat provideri.**

[12] De infirmis **sororibus** tam in **consiliis** quam in cibariis **et** aliis necessariis quae earum requirit infirmitas **teneatur firmiter abbatissa** sollicite **per se et alias sorores inquirere** [13] **et iuxta** possibilitatem **loci caritative et misericorditer providere.** [14] **Quia omnes tenentur** *providere* **et** servire **sororibus suis infirmis** sicut vellent sibi serviri **si ab infirmitate aliqua** teneretur. [15] *Secure manifestet una alteri necessitatem suam,* [16] **et** *si mater diligit et nutrit filiam suam carnalem, quanto diligentius debet* **soror** *diligere et nutrire* **sororem** *suam spiritualem.*

[9] If anything be sent by relatives or if anything else be sent by anyone, the abbess shall have it given her. [10] On her part, if she need it, she may use it, otherwise let her lovingly give it to a sister who does need it.[d] [11] If anyone should have sent her money,[e] let the abbess with the advice of the discreets see that the sister is provided with what she needs.[5]

[12] For the sick sisters, regarding counsel as much as food and the other things which the sick need, the abbess is strictly obliged[6] to be sure to find out, personally and through the other sisters, 13] then, according to the possibilities of the place, to provide for her lovingly and with compassion. [14] For all are bound to provide for and serve their sick sister as they would wish to be served themselves if they were bound by any sickness.[7] [15] Let them confidently reveal their needs to each other.[8] [16] And if a mother loves and nourishes her daughter according to the flesh, how much more lovingly should a sister love and nourish her spiritual sister![9]

---

5   1Reg 8, 2-3; 2Reg 4, 2, 4.
6   Cf. 2Reg 4, 1-3.
7   1Reg 10, 1; 2Reg 6, 11.
8   1Reg 9, 13-14; 2Reg 6, 9-10; 2TestF 3.
9   TestCl 63; BlCl 13; 4LtAg 5.

[17] **Quae infirmae** in saccis cum paleis iaceant et habeant ad caput capitalia cum pluma [18] **et quae indigent** pedulis laneis **et** culcitris **uti possint.**

[19] **Infirmae vero praedictae cum ab introeuntibus monasterium visitantur, possint singulae aliqua bona verba sibi loquentibus breviter respondere.**

[20] **Aliae autem sorores licentiatae monasterium intrantibus loqui non audeant, nisi praesentibus et audientibus duabus discretis sororibus per abbatissam vel eius vicariam assignatis.**

[21] Hanc **formam** loquendi **teneantur pro se** abbatissa **et eius vicaria observare.**

[17] Let the sick lie on pallets of straw and have feather pillows for their heads, [18] and those who need woollen socks and eiderdowns may use them.

[19] Those same sick sisters, when they receive a visit from someone who is visiting the monastery, can briefly respond with good words to each of those who speak with them.^f

[20] The other sisters [although] they have permission to speak to those who enter the monastery, may not do so unless there are two discreet sisters to be present and to listen. These [sisters] are assigned by the abbess or her vicaress.[10]

[21] The abbess and her vicaress are themselves bound to observe this form of speaking.^g

---

10   RegCl 5, 7; 11, 12.

Notes to Chapter Eight

[a] '*Appropriare*' is to be balanced against *sine proprio*, to make one's own as against having nothing of one's own.

[b] In the allegory The Sacred Exchange between Saint Francis and Lady Poverty (c. 1227) in which Francis set out on a pilgrimage to find the Lady Poverty, the two old men he meets in the beginning advise him to 'take some faithful companions endowed with abundant gifts of heaven [v. 11]. Here we also see Clare encouraging her sisters to follow the advice which the Lady Poverty had given Francis and his brothers: to persevere in the things which the Holy Spirit has led you to begin [v.65].

[c] This seems very controlling today but in Clare's time a letter was an expensive item, requiring a parchment which had been professionally prepared. It might also require hiring the services of a scribe or secretary since letters were not normally written by the sender but dictated to a professional letter writer. This is why any treatise on letter writing was called *Ars Dictandi*. In the light of this, we can see that to send a letter secretly was quite a major act of independence and, above all, of appropriation. It might be compared to buying a laptop secretly!

[d] This passage looks back to Augustine who says: *Consequens ergo est ut etiam si quis suis filiis, vel*

aliqua necessitudine ad se pertinentibus, in monasterio constitutis, aliquid contulerit, vel aliquam vestem, sive quodlibet aliud inter necessaria deputandum, non occulte accipiatur, sed sit in potestate praepositi, ut, in rei communi redactum, cui necessarium fuerit, praebeatur – It follows, therefore, that if anyone brings something for their sons or other relatives living in the monastery, whether a garment or anything else they think is needed, this must not be accepted secretly as one's own but must be placed at the disposal of the superior so that, as common property, it can be given to whoever needs it. But if someone secretly keeps something given to him, he shall be judged guilty of theft.

As so often we find Clare taking the substance from the great legislators of the past but giving it her particular touch of warmth and humanity as well as acknowledging the maturity and responsibility of her sisters. For Clare, as for Augustine, it is secrecy which damages the community rather than possession of the material thing itself.

e The word Clare uses here is *pecunia* which means petty cash. Had she meant more serious money the word would have been *denarius*. Like Benedict, she was concerned that the generosity of families should not lead to inequalities among the sisters.

ᶠ The sick sisters, too, have responsibilities to give some 'good word' to their visitors, rather than be passive recipients of other's generosity or regard their visitor as an opportunity to tell them the details of their illness.

ᵍ It is interesting to compare this with the relevant text in Hugolino's Constitutions where he says: *Hanc autem loquendi legem et ipsa abbatissa diligenter custodiat* – Even the abbess herself shall diligently guard this law of speaking (RegHug 6).

Caput IX

[1] *Si qua* **soror contra formam professionis nostrae** *mortaliter inimico instigante peccaverit,* **per abbatissam vel alias sorores bis vel** ter ammonita, [2] **si non emendaverit, quot diebus contumax fuerit tot in terra panem et aquam coram sororibus omnibus in refectorio comedat** [3] **et graviori poenae subiaceat si visum fuerit abbatissae.** [4] **Interim dum contumax fuerit oretur ut Dominus ad poenitentiam cor eius illuminet.**

[5] **Abbatissa vero et eius sorores** *cavere debent ne irascantur vel conturbentur propter peccatum alicuius, quia ira et conturbatio in se et in aliis impediunt caritatem.*
[6] Si contingeret, quod absit, **inter sororem et sororem verbo vel signo occasionem turbationis vel scandali aliquando suboriri** [7] **quae turbationis causam dederit, statim ante quam offerat munus orationis suae coram Domino,**[1] **non solum humiliter prosternat se ad pedes alterius veniam petens,**

---

1   Cf. Mt 5, 23.

On penances for sisters who sin[a]*,
and on the sisters who serve outside the monastery*

9 [1] If any sister, urged by the enemy, sin mortally against the form of our profession, let her be admonished by the abbess or the other sisters two or three times.[2] [2] If she does not amend,[3] then for as many days as she was obstinate let her eat bread and water on the floor in the refectory in front of all the sisters. [3] She may undergo a more severe penance if the abbess thinks it good.[b] [4] While she continues to be obstinate, let her pray that the Lord will enlighten her heart to do penance.

[5] But the abbess and her sisters must take care not to be angry or upset because of the sin of another sister, because anger and upset hinder charity both in oneself and in others.[4]

[6] If it should happen (may it not) that there arise an occasion of disturbance or scandal between sister and sister, either in word or in gesture,[5] [7] let the one who caused the disturbance, at once and before she offers the gift of her prayer in front of the Lord, not only humbly prostrate herself to the ground before the other sister, asking for forgiveness,

---

2   1Reg, 5, 7-8; 2REG, 7, 2.
3   1Reg, 5, 5-6.
4   Adm 11, 3; 1Reg 5, 10; 2REG 7, 5; 1LtF 3.
5   Adm 27, 2.

[8] **verum etiam simpliciter roget, ut pro se intercedat ad Dominum quod sibi indulgeat.** [9] **Illa vero memor illius verbi Domini: nisi ex corde dimiseritis, nec Pater vester caelestis dimittet vobis,**⁶[10] **liberaliter sorori suae omnem iniuriam sibi illatam remittat.**

[11] Sorores servientes extra monasterium longam moram **non** faciant, **nisi causa manifestae necessitatis requirat** [12] **et** *honeste* **debeant ambulare et parum loqui, ut** aedificari **semper** valeant intuentes. [13] **Et** firmiter caveant ne habeant suspecta consortia vel consilia **aliquorum;** [14] nec fiant **commatres** virorum vel mulierem, **ne** hac occasione **murmuratio vel turbatio** oriatur, [15] **nec praesumant rumores** de saeculo **referre in monasterio.** [16] **Et firmiter teneantur de hiis quae intus dicuntur vel aguntur extra monasterium aliquid non referre, quod posset aliquod scandalum generare.**

---

6   Mt 6, 15; 18, 35.

[8] but also with true simplicity let her also ask that the other intercede for her with the Lord so that he be indulgent towards her.[7] [9] And let that other sister[8] bear in mind the words of the Lord: unless you forgive from your heart neither will your heavenly Father forgive you. [10] Let her generously forgive her sister for any injury she may have received.

[11] The sisters who serve outside the monastery[c] should not make any delay unless an obvious need require it.[9] [12] Let them conduct themselves with integrity and speak little,[10] in order to edify those who see them.[d] [13] And let them be particularly careful that they do not have compromising dealings or business[11] with anyone.[e] [14] Let them not be godmothers[12] to men or women lest grumbling and trouble arise because of this.[f] [15] Nor should they presume to repeat secular gossip within the monastery;[13] [16] and they are strictly bound not to repeat outside anything which has been said or done within the monastery that might cause any scandal.[14]

---

7   Adm 20, 4; 24, 3; 1LtF14, 2.
8   1Reg 21, 4-5; Cant 10; PrOF 17.
9   1Reg 2, 9; LtOrd 56.
10   1Reg 11, 1-2; 2Reg 3, 11-12.
11   1Reg 12, 1; 2Reg 11, 2.
12   2Reg 11, 4.
13   Adm 21, 2.
14   LtMin14.

[17] Quod si aliqua **simpliciter in hiis duobus offenderit, sit in providentia abbatissae** misericorditer poenitentiam **sibi** iniungere. [18] **Si autem ex consuetudine vitiosa haberet, iuxta qualitatem culpae abbatissa de consilio discretarum illi poenitentiam iniungat.**

[17] If anyone does, in all simplicity, offend in either of these two things, let the abbess use her judgement with compassion^g to give her some penance.[15] [18] But if this emerges from a sinful habit, the abbess, with the advice of the discreets, shall impose a penance on her according to the fault.

---

15   2Reg 7, 3.

Notes to Chapter Nine

[a] It would have seemed very logical to Clare to follow thoughts on physical illness with those on spiritual sickness.

[b] Cf. the Pre-Narbonne Constitutions 55: *III diebus in pane tantum et aqua ieiunent* – they shall fast for three days on bread and water only. However to understand this directive which does not sit well with our perspective today, we need to know that the Constitutions of the Order of Grandmont (24.4) required forty days on bread and water, the Monastery of St Sixtus in Urbe, Innocent III's foundation in Rome, 'a month' eating *super nudam mensam* – eating on the bare table, which presumably means without a plate or (as was the custom in the Middle Ages) on a trencher, which was a thick slice of bread that served first as plate and then as food – so *super nudam mensam* also implied reduced rations. Eating on the floor for a month was intended to remind them that as they were then physically separated from the community, so – unless they repent as befitted a member of Christ's body – would they be for all eternity: *privabitur perpetuo a sanctorum collegio nisi per dignam poenitentiam denuo facta fuerit membrum Christi.*

^c These sisters should not be simply equated with the institution of lay sisters. Given Clare's profoundly Franciscan insights and absence of any power structures, these sisters are far more likely to have been Clare's version of the 'mothers' in the *Rule for Those Who Live in Hermitages*. There is a body of opinion that the sisters at San Damiano were living by that Rule, while others have suggested that Francis wrote it in the light of what he saw happening at San Damiano. Either way, the ten verses of that Rule contain a number of echoes with Clare's Form of Life. Cf. *Francis' Rule for Hermitages*, an unpublished doctoral thesis by Fr A Raymundo ofm cap, to whom I am indebted for generously sharing with me the chapter on Clare.

^d This is a very real way of fulfilling the fundamental Franciscan calling to 'Rebuild my Church'.

^e Cf. RegInn IV 10: *Et sollicite caveant, ne ad loca suspecta divertant, vel cum personis malae famae familiaritatem habeant* – let them take care not to stray into suspect places or be familiar with people of bad reputation. Clare starts from a basis of trust that the sisters will do nothing inappropriate but seems to have had in mind the thought if not the (apocryphal) words of Francis: Preach the Gospel at all times and use words when you must.

^f It was part of the godparents' task to administer the property of the godchild should they be left parentless or fatherless which, given the high mortality rate, was a common event. To be a godparent was also seen as a way of sealing contracts, resolving enmities and enriching families. In the hands of the less than scrupulous it was easy to enrich oneself from the property of the godchild while they were still a minor. This makes it clear why it was not an appropriate role for one of the sisters.

^g Innocent says on this: *Quod si aliqua contraria fecerit, graviter puniatur* – If one of them does something contrary to this, let her be severely punished.

Caput X

[1] **Abbatissa** *moneat et visitet* **sorores** *suas et humiliter et caritative corrigat eas, non praecipiens aliquid eis quod sit contra animan suam et nostrae* **professionis formam.** [2] **Sorores** *vero subditae recordentur quod propter Deum abnegaverunt proprias voluntates. [3] Unde firmiter suis* **abbatissis** *obedire* **teneantur** *in omnibus quae observare Domino promiserunt et non sunt animae contraria et nostrae* **professioni.** [4] **Abbatissa** *vero tantam familiaritatem habeat circa ipsas ut dicere possint ei et facere sicut dominae* **ancillae** *suae. [5] Nam ita debet esse quod* **abbatissa** *sit omnium* **sororum ancilla.**[1]

[6] *Moneo vero et exhortor in Domino Ihesu Christo, ut caveant* **sorores** *ab omni superbia, vanagloria, invidia, avaritia,*[2] *cura et sollicitudine huius saeculi,*[3] *detractione et murmuratione,* **dissensione et divisione.** [7] **Sint vero sollicitae semper** *invicem* **servare** *mutuae* **dilectionis** unitatem **quae est vinculum perfectionis.**[4]

---

1   Cf. Mt 20, 27.
2   Cf. Lk 12, 15.
3   Cf. Mt 13, 22; Lk 21, 34.
4   Col 3, 14.

Admonition and correction of the sisters

10 [1] The abbess shall admonish and visit[a] her sisters.[5] She shall humbly and lovingly correct them, not commanding them anything against their soul and the form of our profession.[b] [2] But let the sisters who are subject to her[6] remember it is for God that they have renounced their own will.[c] [3] For this reason, they are firmly bound to obey their abbesses in everything which they have promised the Lord to observe, and which is not against their soul and our profession.[d] [4] The abbess however,[7] should be so familiar to them that they can speak and act with her as mistresses do with their handmaid. [5] For this is how it should be, that the abbess be the handmaid of all the sisters.

[6] In the Lord Jesus Christ, I advise and encourage the sisters to beware of all pride, vain glory, jealousy, greed, worry and worldly preoccupation, detraction and murmuring, dissension and division.[8] [7] Instead, let them always be careful to serve each other in the unity of mutual love, for this is the bond of perfection. [9]

---

5 2Reg 10, 2-4.
6 Adm 3, 5; 2Reg 10, 3; TestCl 67.
7 [7] Adm 24, 1; 2Reg 10, 6-7; TestCl 66.
8 1Reg 17, 9; 2Reg 10, 7.
9 RegCl 4, 22.

[8] *Et nescientes litteras non curent litteras discere, [9] sed attendant quod super omnia desiderare debent habere Spiritum Domini et sanctam eius operationem, [10] orare semper ad eum puro corde et habere humilitatem, patientiam in* **tribulatione** *et infirmitate [11] et diligere eos qui nos persecuntur,*[10] *reprehendunt et arguunt, [12] quia dicit Dominus: Beati qui persecutionem patiuntur propter iustitiam, quoniam ipsorum est regnum caelorum.*[11]

[13] *Qui autem perseveraverit usque in finem hic salvus erit.*[12]

---

10   Cf. Mt 5, 4.
11   Cf. Mt 5, 10.
12   Mt 10, 22.

[8] And let those who do not know how to read[e] not be anxious to learn,[13] [9] but let them focus on what they must desire above everything else, which is to have the Spirit of the Lord and his holy working, [10] to pray to him at all times from a pure heart,[14] and to have humility and patience in trouble and sickness. [11] Let them also love those who persecute us, who reprimand us and accuse us [12] because the Lord said: Blessed are those who suffer persecution for justice' sake, for theirs is the kingdom of heaven.[15]

[13] Those who persevere in this until the end shall be saved.[16]

---

13   2Reg 10, 9-12; FTest 25.
14   TestCl 56.
15   1Reg 16, 16; 2Reg10, 14-15.
16   1Reg 16, 23.

Notes to Chapter Ten

a   Clare has taken this directly from Francis' Rule of 1223, in which the itinerant life-style of the brothers explains his use of the verb: to visit. It seems a little strange given that the sisters' were all in one house, but the meaning is clear, that the abbess should make a point of giving time and attention to each sister. It is not enough to smile in the cloister!

b   'Always be lovers of God, of your souls and the souls of your sisters' (BlCl). This chapter presupposes that the sisters are wise lovers of their own souls and ready to see either where they have gone astray or what is inimical to their own particular vocation and gift. Underlying this passage is Francis' Admonition 3. It is also underpinned by *pura sancta simplicitas* – pure, holy simplicity. (SalV, 10.) In this chapter, Clare picks up again on the elements of their withdrawal from society, which had been interrupted at the end of Chapter 5

c   The rather idealised picture in the *Legend of the Three Companions* shows us this in an intense form. (L3C, 42).

d   In Admonition 3, Francis speaks about not losing respect for a prelate who commands something contrary to a brother's conscience; Clare simply says that the abbess is the servant of the sisters. This covers both the integrity of the command and the sisters' freedom to contribute her own insights.

e   Innocent, following Hugolino, says: *si abbatissae visum fuerit, faciat eas litteras edoceri* – if the abbess think fit, she shall be taught to read (RegInn 2). Clare follows Francis and understands that the ability to read in an age when this was unusual also raised a number of other issues which are not simply resolved by the *dictat* of the abbess.

Caput XI

[1] **Hostiaria** sit matura moribus et discreta sitque convenientis aetatis, **quae ibidem in cellula aperta sine hostio in die resideat.** [2] Sit ei et **aliqua** socia idonea **assignata** quae cum necesse fuerit eius vicem in omnibus exsequatur.[a]

[3] Sit autem hostium diversis duabus seris ferreis, valvis et vectibus optime communitum [4] **ut** in nocte maxime duabus clavibus obseretur, **quarum** unam **habeat portanaria** aliam abbatissa, [5] et in die sine custodia minime dimittatur **et** una clave firmiter obseretur.

[6] Caveant autem studiosissime et procurent ne unquam hostium stet apertum, nisi quanto minus fieri poterit congruenter. [7] Nec omnino aperiatur alicui intrare **volenti** nisi cui concessum fuerit a summo pontifice vel a **nostro domino cardinali.**

Keeping the enclosure

11 [1] Let the portress[b] be mature in her behaviour and discreet and of a suitable age. During the day let her stay in an open room without a door.[1] [2] Let her be given a suitable companion who can replace her in everything when necessary.

[3] Let the door[c] be fastened with two separate iron locks, with two well-maintained bolts and bars[2] [4] so that, especially at night, it may be closed with two keys of which the portress has one and the abbess the other. [5] During the day it shall always be closed with one key and never be left without someone responsible.

[6] Let them be most careful to avoid leaving it open without someone responsible, except for the shortest time that can conveniently be done.[3] [7] Nor, absolutely, should they open it to anyone who wants to come in, except those to whom it has been granted by the supreme pontiff, or by our Lord Cardinal.[4]

---

1   RegEr 2.
2   RegCl 5, 11-13.
3   RegEr 9.
4   RegCl 12, 8; 2Reg 11, 1, 3.

[8] **Nec ante solis ortum monasterium ingredi nec post solis occasum sorores intus aliquem remanere permittant, nisi exigente manifesta, rationabili et inevitabili causa.**

[9] Si pro benedictione abbatissae vel pro aliqua sororum in monialem consecranda vel alio etiam modo concessum fuerit alicui episcopo missam interius celebrare, quam a paucioribus et honestioribus poterit sit contentus sociis et ministris. [10] **Cum autem** intra monasterium **ad** opus faciendum necesse fuerit aliquos introire, statuat tunc sollicite abbatissa personam convenientem **ad portam** [11] quae **tantum illis et non aliis** ad opus deputatis aperiat. [12] Caveant studiosissime **omnes** sorores ne tunc **ab ingredientibus** videantur.

[8] Nor should they allow any to enter the monastery before sunrise[d] nor to remain there after sunset[5] unless there be a need which is obvious, reasonable and unavoidable.[6]

[9] If, for the blessing of an abbess[e] or for the consecration of any sister or some similar purpose, a bishop celebrate Mass inside [the cloister], let him be content with the smallest possible number of companions and ministers and the most trustworthy. [10] If it becomes necessary for anyone to enter the monastery to do some work, the abbess shall carefully settle who is the best person to be at the door.[f] [11] Let her only open to those appointed to the work and to nobody else. [12] Let the sisters be very careful that they are not seen by those who come in.[7]

---

5   RegCl 2, 13.
6   RegCl 5, 14.
7   RegCl 8, 20.

Notes to Chapter Eleven

a Cf. RegSB 66, 2-5.

b Almost the whole of this chapter looks back to the Rules of Hugolino and Innocent with some more gentle touches from Benedict. For instance in verse 1, Innocent says the portress must *Deum timeat* - fear God, while Benedict (followed by Clare) simply indicates that she must be mature and discreet. Most of what Clare lays down is in Innocent, but not all of Innocent is in Clare. To penetrate her thinking on cloister, we do well to read her words in the light of what she omitted as well as what she said. Much of the change is in her positive, trusting attitude, to an extent which was unusual in an era where women remained minors in law for their whole lives and were officially considered more prone to sin than men.

c Presumably this means the main door, since the portress' room has no door.

d Clare is very insistent on silence in the house from sunset to sunrise, suggesting that perhaps many people came to San Damiano seeking help, cures, counsel, food etc. There must have been a real need to ensure that the contemplative life of the sisters did not lose depth in consequence.

e   Again Hugolino and Innocent are less generous in their permissions: *Quod si forte* – if by chance, they both say (RegHug 10, RegInn 6), 'If by chance permission is ever given to some Bishop . . . (RegHug).

f   Here as elsewhere we are reminded of small town politics and that the sisters, drawn from all levels of society, probably had relatives and friends among those who came to the monastery. Clare retains freedom to make decisions here, since the best person to open the door could, in humanity and compassion, be the sister of the workman!

Caput XII

[1] Visitator **noster sit semper** de ordine fratrum minorum **secundum voluntatem et mandatum nostri cardinalis** [2] **et sit** talis de cuius **honestate** et moribus plena notitia habeatur. [3] **Cuius officium erit** tam in capite quam in membris corrigere excessus **commissos contra formam professionis nostrae.** [4] **Qui stans in loco publico ut videri ab aliis possit** cum pluribus **et singulis loqui liceat** quae ad visitationis officium pertinent **secundum quod melius viderit expedire.**

[5] Capellanum **etiam cum uno socio clerico** bonae famae discretionis providae **et duos fratres laicos sanctae conversationis et honestatis amatores** [6] in subsidium paupertatis nostrae, sicut misericorditer a praedicto ordine fratrum minorum semper habuimus [7] **intuitu pietatis Dei et beati Francisci ab eodem ordine de gratia postulamus.** [8] **Non liceat** capellano **sine socio** monasterium **ingredi.** [9] **Et intrantes in loco sint publico, ut** se possint **alterutrum** semper **et ab aliis intueri.** [10] **Pro confessione** infirmarum **quae** ad

The visitator, the chaplain, the cardinal protector

12 [1] Let our visitator always be of the Order of Friars Minor[1] according to the will and command of our cardinal, [2] and let him be someone of whom the cardinal well knows both his integrity and his conduct. [3] It will be his task to correct excesses committed against the form of our profession,[2] in the head as much as in the members.[a] [4] Standing in a public place where he can be seen by all, he can speak, as seems best to him, both to many as well as to individuals about that which concerns his visitation.[b]

[5] We have always had a chaplain and a cleric companion of good reputation and prudent discretion, and two lay brothers[c] of holy conversation and lovers of integrity [6] to support our poverty and as a mercy from the same Order of Friars Minor, [7] and through the tenderness of God and of blessed Francis we ask them from the same Order as a grace. [8] The chaplain shall not be allowed to enter the monastery without a companion.[3] [9] When he has entered, let him stay in public so as to see and be seen by others. [10] He may

---

1   RegCl 6, 4-5.
2   RegCl 2, 34; 9, 1; TestCl 51.
3   RegCl 11, 7; 2Reg 11, 3.

locutorium **ire non possent, pro communicandis eisdem, pro extrema unctione, pro** animae commendatione **liceat eisdem intrare.** [11] **Pro** exequiis **vero et missarum sollempniis defunctarum et** ad fodiendam vel aperiendam sepulturam seu **etiam** coaptandam **possint sufficientes et** idonei **de abbatissae providentia** introire.

[12] Ad haec **sorores firmiter teneantur semper habere illum** de sanctae romanae ecclesiae cardinalibus **pro nostro** gubernatore, protectore et correctore, qui fuerit a domino papa **fratribus minoribus** deputatus, [13] ut semper subditae et subiectae pedibus eiusdem sanctae ecclesiae stabiles in fide[4] catholica, paupertatem et humilitatem Domini nostri Ihesu Christ **et eius sanctissimae Matris** et sanctum evangelium, quod firmiter promisimus, **in perpetuum** observemus. **Amen.**

---

4   Cf. Col 1, 23.

come in for the confessions of the sick who are unable to go to the parlour,⁵ to give them communion, extreme unction and the commendation of their souls. [11] For the services and solemn Masses for the dead, for closing or opening a grave or even to arrange it, a competent and suitable individual can come in at the discretion of the abbess.

[12] For these reasons, the sisters are firmly bound always to have for our governor, protector and corrector,⁶ that cardinal of the Roman Church whom the Lord Pope will have established for the Friars Minor.ᵈ [13] This is because, always subject and prostrate at the feet of that same holy Church, stable in the Catholic faith, let us observe for ever the poverty and humility of our Lord Jesus Christ and of his most holy Mother,⁷ and the holy Gospel which we have firmly promised. Amen.ᵉ

---

5   RegCl 3, 15.
6   2Reg 12, 4-5; 1TestF 39; TestCl 44.
7   RegCl 6, 7; 1TestF 41; BlCl 15.

Notes to Chapter Twelve

[a] Cf. Pre-Narbonne Constitutions 20: *Visitatores iuxta formam premissam corrigant fratrum excessos quos visitabunt* – According to the aforesaid form, the visitator shall correct any excesses in the brothers whom he visits. Innocent says that he shall come for 'correction and reform' (RegInn 8).

[b] Cf. Pre-Narbonne Constitutions 19: *Teneantur fratres visitatoribus suis in his quae ad offitium visitationis pertinent et non in aliis obedire* – The brothers are bound to obey the visitator in those things which pertain to his visitation and not in anything else.

[c] Clare must have known that the 1239 Chapter of the friars limited the number of lay brethren who could be accepted. Was this a way of saying she wanted brothers who had been with Francis from the beginning? By 1260, the Chapter of Narbonne would require special permission from the Minister General for anyone to enter as a lay brother. This was all part of the growing clericalisation of the Order.

[d] For many years the Cardinal Protector had been Hugolino and at the time when Clare was writing the office was held by Rainaldo, later to be Alexander IV. On the whole it must have been a good experience to enable Clare to write so positively about the protector

and his task in their regard. The office of 'visitator and corrector' went back to Francis who asked for Hugolino to adopt this role and himself also appointed one of the brothers to fulfil this task for those 'virgins and widows [who] struck by their preaching, on their advice secluded themselves in cities and towns in monasteries established for doing penance' (L3C 60). This office of Cardinal Protector lasted until 1908 when it was replaced by the Sacred Congregation for Institutes of Consecrated Life.

c The Form of Life of Clare begins and ends with the same words as the Rule of Francis, with the addition of *in perpetuum* – let us observe forever.

The Testament

The Authenticity of the Testament

Questions about the authenticity of the Testament of Clare are not new and are based on four factors:

1. The absence of a manuscript tradition. Until recently the earliest known text was in Wadding's Annales Minorum of 1628, which text he received, he says vaguely, *ex memoriali antiquo* which roughly means 'from of old. His authority was accepted by both the Bolandists in 1735 and the friars of Quaracchi in 1897;

2. The style being different from either the Letters or the Rule

3. The Testament mentions the Privilege of Poverty of Innocent III of which no manuscript has been found;

4. There is no known mention of a Testament of Clare until the Perugian reform of 1445.

However, during the early 1900s scholarly opinion turned in favour of authenticity, especially since some older manuscripts have come to light, notably in Messina and Urbino, of which Messina seems to be the oldest.

The Messina Manuscript is a 14th century copy belonging to Bl Eustochia Calafato, a 15th century Poor Clare in

Messina who was a close friend of Sr Cecilia Coppola, Abbess of Perugia and leader of the Perugian reform of 1445. We do not know how this m/s came into the hands of Sr Cecilia but it is more likely to have been she who gave it to Bl Eustochia than the legendary tale that it was found on the bank of a Spanish river by a passing nobleman.

In the Messina manuscript are the Form of Life, the Privilege of Poverty of Innocent III, *Solet annuere* of Innocent IV, the Testament and the Blessing of Clare. Some notable scholars, primarily the highly respected Attilio Bartoli-Angeli, a paleographer, are of the opinion that this manuscript is in the handwriting of Br Leo. Bartoli-Langeli suggests that after Clare's death, the brothers and sisters sat together to recall her main concerns and advice, resulting in a text which we now call the Testament. Others however indicate the aptness of this discovery for validating the reform movement.

The Uppsala manuscript is now in Vadstena, Sweden and contains the Form of Life, the Privilege of Poverty of Innocent III, the Testament and the Blessing.

The authenticity of the Privilege of Poverty of Innocent III and with it the Testament have been strongly contested by a German Capuchin, a historian of canon law, Werner Malaczek.[1] He is convinced both texts emerged from the Perugia reform and suggests that Sr Cecilia herself wrote the text to give the reform credibility in an age when copyright did not exist and authenticity was less literally understood. Malaczek's arguments are scholarly, compelling and well argued and a number of reputable scholars believe he is right.

At the moment the jury is out. If the Testament is *by Clare*, then Malaczek's argument still has to be answered; if by a group of *friars and sisters* after Clare's death, as a kind of posthumous last letter, then supporting evidence is required; if it came from *the reform* of 1445, then further research may bring this to light. Whatever its origin, it is of great value as an early Franciscan document challenging us on vocation and fidelity.

---

1   Werner Malaczek, "Questions about the Authenticity of the Privilege of Poverty of Innocent III and of the Testament of Clare of Assisi", Greyfriars Review Supplement 12 (1998), pp. 1-80.

Testamentum

[1] In nomine Domini. Amen.

[2] Inter alia beneficia,[2] quae a largitore nostro *Patre misericordiarum*[3] recepimus et cotidie recipimus et unde Christi glorioso Patri gratiarum actiones magis agere debemus, [3] est de vocatione nostra, quae quanto perfectior et maior est, tanto magis illi plus debemus. [4] Unde apostolus: *Agnosce vocationem tuam*.[4] [5] Factus est pro nobis Filius Dei *via*,[5] quam *verbo* et *exemplo* ostendit et docuit[6] nos beatissimus pater noster Franciscus, verus amator et imitator ipsius.

[6] Igitur considerare debemus, sorores dilectae, immensa beneficia Dei in nobis collata, [7] sed inter cetera, quae per servum suum dilectum patrem nostrum beatum Franciscum in nobis Deus dignatus est operari, [8] non solum post conversionem nostram, sed etiam dum essemus in saeculi misera vanitate. [9] Nam cum ipse sanctus adhuc non habens fratres nec socios, statim quasi post conversionem suam,

---

2   Col 3, 17
3   2Cor14 1, 3.
4   Cf. 1Cor15. 1, 26.
5   Cf. Jn 14, 6.
6   Cf. 1Tim 4, 12.

The Testament

[1] In the name of the Lord. Amen

[2]Among the other benefits which we have received (and receive daily) from the largesse of our Father of mercies, and for which we must above all give thanks to the glorious Father of Christ,[7] [3] is that of our vocation. In so far as this is greater and more perfect, then so much the more must we do so.[8] [4] Therefore the Apostle: Know your vocation.[9] [5] The Son of God was made the way for us, which by word and example our most blessed father Francis, a true lover and his imitator, showed and taught us.

[6] Therefore, beloved sisters, we must ponder on the immense good gifts of God conferred on us, [7] but among the rest is that which God chose to be worked in us through His beloved servant our father blessed Francis, [8] not only after our conversion but even while we were in the miserable emptiness of the world. [9] For when the saint himself, almost immediately after his conversion and still without brothers or companions,

7   vv. 22, 58.
8   Adm 5, 1; 26, 3-4; 2LtF 30.
9   Cf. Sermon of Pope St Leo the Great, *In Nativitate Domini*, 3.

[10] cum ecclesiam Sancti Damiani aedificaret, ubi consolatione divina totaliter visitatus, compulsus est saeculum ex toto relinquere, [11] prae magna laetitia et illustratione Spiritus Sancti de nobis prophetavit, quod Dominus postea adimplevit

[12] Ascendens enim tunc temporis super murum dictae ecclesiae, quibusdam pauperibus, ibi iuxta morantibus, alta voce lingua francigena loquebatur: [13] Venite et adiuvate me in opere monasterii Sancti Damiani, [14] quoniam adhuc erunt dominae ibi, quarum famosa vita et conversatione sancta *glorificabitur* Pater noster *caelestis[10]* in universa ecclesia sua sancta.

[15] In hoc ergo considerare possumus copiosam benignitatem Dei in nobis, [16] qui propter abundantem misericordiam et caritatem suam de nostra *vocatione et electione[11]* per sanctum suum dignatus est ista loqui. [17] Et non solum de nobis ista pater noster beatissimus Franciscus prophetavit, sed etiam de aliis, quae venturae erant in vocatione sancta, in qua Dominus nos vocavit.

---

10   Cf. Mt. 5, 16.
11   Cf. 2Pt. 1, 10.

[10] while he was rebuilding the church of San Damiano, where he was totally overwhelmed by divine consolation and was driven wholly to leave the world,[12] [11] through the great joy and enlightenment of the Holy Spirit, prophesied about us that which the Lord later fulfilled.

[12] For at that time, climbing onto the wall of the said church, he spoke in a loud voice in the French language to certain poor people who were living nearby: [13] 'Come and help me in the work of the monastery of San Damiano[13] [14] for there will be ladies there whose famous life and holy conduct will glorify our heavenly Father in in all His holy Church.'

[15] In this therefore we are able to reflect on the overflowing kindness of God towards us [16] who, because of His abundant mercy and love for our vocation and election chose to speak about it in this way through His saint. [17] And our most blessed father Francis not only prophesied this about us but also about who were to come in the holy vocation to which the Lord has called us.[14]

---

12   1TestF 4.
13   vv. 30-13.
14   AudPov 1.

[18] Quanta ergo sollicitudine quantoque studio mentis et corporis mandata Dei et patris nostri servare debemus ut cooperante Domino *talentum*[15] multiplicatum reddamus! [19] Ipse enim Dominus non solum posuit nos ut formam aliis in exemplum et speculum, sed etiam sororibus nostris, quas ad vocationem nostram Dominus advocabit, [20] ut et ipsae sint conversantibus in mundo in speculum et exemplum. [21] Cum igitur nos vocaverit Dominus ad tam magna, ut in nobis se valeant speculari quae aliis in speculum sunt et exemplum, [22] tenemur multum benedicere Deum et laudare et ad benefaciendum in Domino confortari amplius. [23] Quapropter, si secundum formam praedictam vixerimus, *exemplum* nobile aliis *relinquemus*[16] et aeternae beatitudinis *bravium*[17] labore brevissimo acquiremus.

[24] Postquam altissimus Pater caelestis per misericordiam suam et gratiam cor meum dignatus est illustrare, ut exemplo et doctrina beatissimi patris nostri Francisci poenitentiam facerem,

---

15   Cf. Mt 25, 25-23.
16   Cf. 2Mc 6, 28 and 31.
17   Cf. Phil 3, 14.

[18]So with what care and how much attention of mind and body must we observe the commands of God and our father, so that with the Lord's help we may give back an increase of talents![18] [19] For the Lord Himself has not only placed us as a pattern to others for an example and a mirror,[19] but even to our sisters whom the Lord will call into our vocation, [20] so that they may be a mirror and an example to those living in the world. [21] When, therefore, the Lord has called us to such greatness, that those who are a mirror and example to others are well mirrored in us, [22] we must greatly bless the Lord, and give praise, and be even more strengthened to do good in the Lord.[20] [23] This is why, if we shall have lived according to the above way, we will leave a noble example to others and by a very short labour, gain the prize of eternal blessedness.

[24] After the most high heavenly Father,[21] through His mercy and grace, chose to flood my heart with light so that I should do penance according to the example and teaching of our most blessed father Francis,[22]

---

18   1LtF 13, 12.
19   4LtAg 15-24.
20   v. 2; Cant 15.
21   v. 34; RegCl 6, 1.
22   1TestF 1.

[25] paolo post conversionem ipsius, una cum paucis sororibus quas Dominus mihi dederat paolo post conversionem meam, obedientiam voluntarie sibi promisi, [26] sicut Dominus lumen gratiae suae nobis contulerat per eius vitam mirabilem et doctrinam.

[27] Attendens autem beatus Franciscus quod essemus fragiles et debiles secundum corpus, nullam tamen necessitatem, paupertatem, laborem, tribulationem vel vilitatem et contemptum saeculi recusabamus, [28] immo pro magnis deliciis reputabamus sicut exemplis sanctorum et fratrum suorum examinaverat nos frequenter, gavisus est multum in Domino; [29] et ad pietatem erga nos motus, obligavit se nobis per se et per religionem suam habere semper de nobis tamquam de fratribus suis curam diligentem et sollicitudinem specialem.

[30] Et sic de voluntate Dei et beatissimi patris nostri Francisci ivimus ad ecclesiam Sancti Damiani moraturae, [31] ubi Dominus in brevi tempore per misericordiam suam et gratiam nos multiplicavit, ut impleretur quod Dominus praedixerat per sanctum suum.

[25] a little while after his conversion, together with the few sisters whom the Lord had given me a little after my own conversion, I freely promised him obedience[23] [26] in the the same way, since through his wonderful life and teaching the Lord had drawn us into the light of His grace. [27] Blessed Francis realised that we were fragile and physically weak but that we refused no necessity, poverty, labour, trouble or powerlessness or the scorn of the world,[24] [28] and indeed we considered these to be great delights according to the examples of the saints and of his brothers, then he frequently examined us and was greatly delighted in the Lord. [29] And so, moved to tenderness for us, he committed himself to us both for himself and for his Order[25] always to have for us, just as for his brothers, a loving attention and special concern.[26] [30] And so, by the will of God and of our most blessed father Francis, we went to stay in the church of San Damiano.[27] [31] There in a short time the Lord multiplied us through His mercy and grace[28] so that

---

23   1Reg 12, 3; 1TestF 4.

24   RegCl 6, 2; 1LtAg 22; 3LtAg 38-39.

25   Since 1220 the friars had been considered an Order, but presumably Clare uses the older word which represents the position of the brotherhood at the time of which she was speaking. It has been translated as *Order* here because we do not use *religion* in that way in English.

26   v. 49; RegCl 6, 4.

27   v. 14.

28   AudPov 1.

[32] Nam antea steteramus in loco alio, licet parum.

[33] Postea scripsit nobis formam vivendi et maxime ut in sancta paupertate semper perseveraremus. [34] Nec fuit contentus in vita sua nos *hortari multis sermonibu*s[29] et exemplis ad amorem sanctissimae paupertatis et observentiam eiusdem, sed plura scripsit nobis tradidit, ne post mortem suam ullatenus declinaremus ab ipsa, [35] sicut et Dei Filius, dum vixit in mundo, ab ipsa sancta paupertate numquam voluit declinare. [36] Et beatissimus pater noster Franciscus, *eius vestigia*[30] imitatus, sanctam paupertatem suam, quam eligit per se et per suos fratres, exemplo suo et doctrina, dum vixit ab ipsa nullatenus declinavit.

[37] Considerans igitur, ego Clara, Christi et sororum pauperum monasterii Sancti Damiani ancilla, licet indigna, et plantula sancti patris, cum aliis meis sororibus, tam altissimam professionem nostram et tanti patris mandatum, [38] fragilitatem quoque aliarum, quam timebamus in nobis post obitum sancti patris nostri

---

29   Cf. Acts 20, 1.
30   Cf. 1Pet 2, 21.

what the Lord had foretold through His saint would be fulfilled.

[32] Before then we had stayed in another place but not for long.

[33] After that he wrote us a Form for Living and above all that we should always persevere in holy poverty.[31] [34] Nor was he content during his life to encourage us[32] with many words and examples to love most holy poverty and to observe the same, but he handed us many writings, lest after his death we should fall away from her in any respect [35] just as the Son of God, while He lived in the world, wanted never to fall away from this holy poverty. [36] And our most blessed father Francis,[33] imitating the least trace of Him,[a] never wanted while he lived to fall away from his holy poverty which he had chosen for himself and his brothers, as he showed by his example and teaching.

[37] I, Clare, therefore, the handmaid of Christ and the poor sisters of the monastery of San Damiano,[34] (although unworthy) and the little plant[35] of the holy father, together with my other sisters, considering our most high profession and the command of such a father [38] and considering the fragility of others which we feared in ourselves after the death of our holy father Francis who

31   RegCl Prol 4-5; 6, 3-4.
32   vv. 24, 46; RegCl 6, 7-9; UltVol. 1-3.
33   RB, 6, 2-3; FrTst 28-29; UltVol 1.
34   v. 48; RegCl 1, 3; BlCl 6; 1LtAg 2; 4LtAg 2.
35   Cf. RegCl 1, 3; 2Cel 109.

Francisci, qui erat *columna* nostra et unica consolatio post Deum et *firmamentum*[36] [39] iterum atque iterum voluntarie nos obligavimus dominae nostrae sanctissimae paupertati, ne post mortem meam sorores, quae sunt et quae venturae sunt, ab ipsa valeant ullatenus declinare.

[40] Et sicut ego studiosa et sollicita semper fui sanctam paupertatem, quam Domino et patri nostro beato Francisco promisimus observare et ab aliis facere observari, [41] sic teneantur usque in finem illae quae mihi succedent in officio sanctam paupertatem cum Dei auxilio observare et facere observari. [42] Immo etiam ad maiorem cautelam sollicita fui a domino papa Innocentio, sub cuius tempore coepimus, et ab aliis successoribus suis nostram professonem sanctissimae paupertatis, quam Domino et beato patri nostro promisimus, eorum privilegiis facere roborari, [43] ne aliquo tempore ab ipsa declinaremus ullatenus.

---

36   Cf. 1Tim. 3, 15.

was our pillar and, after God, our sole consolation,[37] and our foundation, [39] we freely committed ourselves again and again to our lady, most holy poverty, lest after my death the sisters, those now and those to come, should fall away from her in any respect.[38]

[40]And just as I was always eager and careful to observe, and to enable others to observe,[39] the holy poverty which we had promised the Lord and our father blessed Francis, [41] so those who will succeed me in office shall be bound until the end,[40] to observe and to enable holy poverty to be observed with the help of God.[41] [42] What is more, for an even greater precaution,[42] I was careful to have our profession of the most holy poverty which we had promised to the Lord and to our blessed father, made strong with privileges by the Lord Pope Innocent[b] in whose time we began, and by others of his successors,[43] [43] lest at any time we fall away from it in any respect.[44]

---

37 RegCl 4, 12.
38 1TestF 29; RegCl 6, 10-13.
39 RegCl 6, 10; BlCl 15.
40 2LtF 51.
41 RegCl 6, 10-11.
42 RegCl Prol 8; 6, 10.
43 Gregory IX.
44 v. 35.

[44] Quapropter, flexis genibus et utroque homine inclinato, sanctae matri Ecclesiae Romanae, summo pontifici et praecipue domino cardinali, qui religioni Fratrum Minorum et nobis fuerit deputatus, recommendo omnes sorores meas quae sunt et quae venturae sunt,

> [45] ut amore illius Dei,
> qui pauper positus est in praesepio[45]
> pauper vixit in saeculo
> et nudus remansit in patibulo,

[46] semper *gregi* suo *pusillo*,[46] quem Dominus Pater genuit in Ecclesia sua sancta, verbo et exemplo beatissimi patris nostri sancti Francisci insequendo paupertatem et humilitatem dilecti Filii sui et gloriosae Virginis matris suae, [47] sanctam paupertatem, quam Deo et beatissimo patri nostro sancto Francisco promisimus, faciat observari et in ipsa dignetur fovere ipsas semper et conservare.

---

45   Lk 2, 12.
46   Cf. Lk 12, 32.

[44] This is why, on bended knee and prostrate in body and soul[c] I recommend all my sisters, both those now and those to come, to the holy mother Church of Rome, to the supreme Pontiff and especially to the Lord Cardinal who has been assigned to the Order[47] of Friars Minor and to us;

> [45] so that for love of this God
> who poor was placed in a crib,
> poor, lived in the world
> and naked was on the gibbet,

[46] they may always encourage and preserve the little flock which the Lord Father begot in His holy Church through the word and example of our most blessed father Saint[d] Francis in following the poverty and humility of His beloved Son and the glorious Virgin His mother. May they always enable us to observe the holy poverty which we have promised to God and our most blessed father Saint Francis.[e]

---

47   See footnote 25 above about Order and Religion.

[48] Et sicut Dominus dedit nobis beatissimum patrem nostrum Franciscum in fundatorem, plantatorem et adiutorem nostrum in servitio Christi et in his quae Domino et beato patri nostro promisimus, [49] qui etiam dum vixit sollicitus fuit verbo et exemplo semper excolere et fovere nos, plantulam suam, [50] sic recommendo et relinquo sorores meas, quae sunt et quae venturae sunt, successori beatissimi patris nostri Francisci et toti religioni, [51] ut sint nobis in adiutorium proficiendi semper in melius ad serviendum Deo et observandam praecipue melius sanctissimam paupertatem.

[52] Si vero contingeret aliquo tempore dictas sorores locum dictum relinquere et ad alium se transferre, praedictam formam paupertatis, quam Deo et beatissimo patri nostro Francisco promisimus, post mortem meam ubicumque fuerint, observare nihilominus teneantur.

[48] And just as the Lord gave us our most blessed father Francis as founder,[48] planter and our helper in the service of Christ and in these things which we have promised the Lord and our blessed father, [49] who even while he lived was always careful to tend and cherish us, his little plant, by word and example, [50] in the same way, I recommend and leave my sisters, those now and those to come,[49] to the successors of our most blessed father Francis and to the whole Order, [51] that they always be a help to us in reaching for the best in our service of God and even more so in a better observance of most holy poverty.

[52] However, if it should happen that at some time the said sisters leave the said place and transfer themselves to another, they too are likewise bound, after my death and wherever they shall be, to observe the said form of poverty which we have promised God and our most blessed father Francis.

---

48   v. 37; RegCl 1, 3; BlCl 6. Surely this thought connects with the one of Care and the early brothers as plants whom Francis the Planter planted.

49   RegCl 1, 4-5.

[53] Sit tamen sollicita et providens tam illa, quae erit in officio, quam aliae sorores, ne circa supradictum locum de terra acquirant vel recipiant, nisi quantum extrema necessitas pro horto ad excolenda olera poposcit. [54] Si autem ab aliqua parte pro honestate et remotione monasterii, ex saepta horti opporteret plus haberi de terra, non permittant plus acquiri vel etiam recipiant, nisi quantum extrema necessitas poscit. [55] Et illa terra penitus non laboreturnec seminatur, sed semper solida et inculta permaneat.

[56] Moneo et exhortor in Domino Iesu Christo omnes sorores meas, quae sunt et quae venturae sunt, ut semper studeant imitari viam sanctae simplicitatis, humilitatis, paupertatis ac etiam honestatem sanctae conversationis, [57] sicut ab initio nostrae conversionis a Christo edoctae sumus et a beatissimo patre nostro beato Francisco. [58] Ex quibus, non nostris meritis, sed sola misericordia et gratia largitoris, ipse *Pater misericordiarum*,[50] tam his qui longe sunt quam his qui prope sunt, bonae famae sparsit *odorem*.[51]

---

50   2Cor. 1, 3.
51   Cf. 2Cor. 2, 15.

[53] Let them be careful and far-sighted, both the one who will be in office and the other sisters, lest they acquire or receive land around the aforesaid place beyond what extreme necessity demands for a garden in which to grow vegetables. [54] But if, on the other hand, for the integrity [of the life] and the apartness of the monastery, they need to have more land than a vegetable garden, they are not permitted to acquire or even to receive more than extreme necessity demands.[52] [55] And that land may not be worked or sown but always stay fallow and uncultivated.

[56] In the Lord Jesus Christ,[53] I remind and encourage all my sisters, those now and those to come,[54] that they always study how to imitate the way of holy simplicity, humility, poverty and, indeed, the totality of a holy way of life. [57] This is how we were taught at the beginning of our conversion by Christ and by our most blessed father blessed Francis. [58] Because of this,[55] and not through our merits but only through the largesse of His mercy and grace,[56] the Father of mercies himself always spread the fragrance of good repute, as much for those who were far away as for those who were near.

---

52   RegCl 6, 14-15.
53   2Reg 2, 10.
54   1Reg 17, 15; 2Reg 10, 11; RegCl 10, 10.
55   v. 2.
56   1LtF 10, 9; 1LtAg 3.

[59] Et ex caritate Christi invicem diligentes, amorem, quem intus habetis, foris per opera demonstretis,[57] [60] ut ex hoc exemplo provocatae sorores semper crescant in amorem Dei et in mutuam caritatem,

[61] Rogo etiam illam quae erit in officio sororum, ut magis studeat praeesse aliis virtutibus et sanctis moribus quam officio, [62] quatenus eius exemplo provocatae sorores suae, non tantum ex officio obediant, sed potius ex amore. [63] Sit etiam provida et discreta circa sorores suas, sicut bona mater ergo filias suas, [64] et praecipue ut de eleemosynis quas Dominus dabit, eis secundum necessitatem uniuscuiusque studeat providere. [65] Sit etiam benigna et communis, ut secure possint manifestare necessitates suas, [66] et recurrere ad eam omni hora confidenter, sicut eis videbitur expedire, tam pro se quam pro sororibus suis.

[67] Sorores vero quae sunt subditae recordentur quod propter Deum abnegaverunt proprias voluntates. [68] Unde volo quod obediant suae matri, sicut promiserunt Domino, sua spontanea voluntate, [69] ut mater earum videns caritatem,

---

57   Cf. Jas 2, 18.

[59] And holding each other dear in the love of Christ, let that love which you have for one another within be shown outwardly in deeds.[58] [60] Then the sisters, challenged by this example, may always grow in the love of God and in loving esteem for each other.

[61] In addition I ask of the one who will hold office among the sisters that she strive to go before the others more by virtues and holy behaviour than by office.[59] [62] Let her example challenge her sisters so that they do not obey the office but the love. [63] Let her be far-sighted and discreet about her sisters, as a good mother is towards her daughters. [64] Above all, let her be careful that out of the alms the Lord will give, she provide according to the needs of each one. [65] Let her be so kindly and ordinary that they are safe to reveal their needs[60] [66] and confident to come back to her at any time, if it seem expedient, as much for themselves as for their sisters.

[67] However, let the sisters who are subject[61] remember that because of God they have set their own wills aside.[62] [68] For this reason, I want them to obey their mother as they have promised God, of their own free will.[63] [69] Then their mother, seeing the love, humility

---

58   Adm 9, 3; 1Reg 11, 5; RegCl 4, 22
59   RegCl 4, 9.
60   1Ref 6, 8; RegCl 8, 15.
61   2Reg 10, 3; RegCl 10, 2.
62   2Reg 10, 2; RegCl 10, 2.
63   RegCl 1, 5.

humilitatem et unitatem quam invicem habent, omne onus quod de offico tolerat, levius portet, [70] et quod molestum est et amarum, propter earum sanctam conversationem, ei in dulcedinem convertatur.

[71] Et quoniam *arcta est via* et semita, et *angusta est porta* per quam itur et intrantur *ad vitam, et pauci sunt qui*⁶⁴ ambulant et intrant per *eam*. [72] Et si aliqua sunt qui ad tempus ambulant per eam, paucissimi sunt qui perseverant in ea. [73] Beati vero quibus datum est *ambulare* per eam et *perseverare usque in finem.*⁶⁵

[74] Caveamus ergo, quod si per viam Domini intravimus, quod culpa nostra et ignorantia, aliquo tempore ab ipsa nullatenus declinemus, [75] ne tanto Domino et suae Virgini matri et patri nostro beato Francisco, Ecclesiae triumphanti et etiam militanti iniuriam deferamus. [76] Scriptum est: *Maledicti qui declinant a mandatis tuis.*⁶⁶

---

64   Cf. Mt. 7, 14.
65   Cf. Ps. 118, 1; Mt. 10, 22.
66   Ps. 118, 21.

and unity[67] which they have among themselves, will more lightly carry every burden of her office. [70] Then what was irksome and bitter will be changed into sweetness for her because of their holy way of life.[68]

[71] And because the way is straight as is the path, and because the gate through which one goes out and in to life is narrow,[69] there are few who walk and enter by that gate. [72] And if there are some who walk that way for a while, there are very few who persevere in it. [73] Blessed indeed the one to whom it is given both to walk in it and to persevere until the end.

[74] Let us take care,[70] then, lest having entered on the way of the Lord we fall away from it at any time through our fault and ignorance, [75] and lest we injure such a Lord and His Virgin mother,[71] and our father blessed Francis, the Church triumphant and even the Church militant.[72] [76] For it is written: Cursed are those who fall away from Your commandments.[73]

---

67 LtElias 3-6; RegCl 4, 9.
68 2TestF 3.
69 1Reg 11, 10-11; 1LtAg 29.
70 v. 35.
71 BlCl 9-10.
72 1Reg 5, 19; 1LtF 3, 2; LtR 4-5.
73 BlCl 7.

[77] *Huius rei gratia flecto genua mea ad Patrem Domini nostri Iesu Christi,*[74] suffragantibus meritis gloriosae Virginis sanctae Mariae matris eius et beatissimi patris nostri Francisci et omnium sanctorum, [78] ut et ipse Dominus, qui dedit bonum principium,[75] *det incrementum,*[76] det etiam finalem perseverantiam. Amen.

[79] Hoc scriptum, ut melius debeat observari, relinquo vobis, carissimis et dilectis sororibus meis, praesentibus et venturis, in signum benedictionis Domini et beatissimi patris nostri Francisci et benedictionis meae, matris et ancillae vestrae.

Explicit testamentum beatae Clarae virginis.

---

74   Eph 3, 14.
75   Cf. 2Cor 8, 6 and 11.
76   1Cor 3, 6 -7.

[77] For this reason, I bend my knees to the Father of our Lord Jesus Christ, helped by the merits of the glorious Virgin, holy Mary His mother, of our most blessed father Francis and all the saints, [78] that the Lord Himself, who has given a good beginning, will give growth and, indeed, will give final perseverance. Amen.

[79] I leave this writing to you, my dearest and chosen sisters, those now and those to come, so that it may be better observed as a sign of the Lord's blessing and that of our most blessed father Francis and of my blessing, that of your mother and handmaid.

The end of the Testament of blessed Clare, the virgin.[77]

---

77   Not in all manuscripts.

Notes to the Testament

[a] *Vestigia* – vestiges, a word which was to become significant to Bonaventure's spiritual teaching.

[b] Innocent III. This unambiguous reference is one of the reasons why the Testament's authenticity is linked with that of the Privilege of Poverty. Once the authenticity of the latter was questioned, then the Testament was also implicated. Should the Testament definitely be in the hand-writing of Brother Leo, then this argument will need radical revision. It is, however, always possible that Innocent III gave Clare a verbal 'privilege' in the same way as he verbally gave Francis his *propositum* in 1209. This would have been quite consistent with Innocent's policies towards the new evangelical groups of the time.

[c] Latin: *utroque homine inclinato*, bowing both of man [lit.]. It seems Clare has in mind Francis' use of *intus et foris*, [FtTest 41] within and without. Body and soul is clearly her meaning, cf. 1Cel 45 and 101·

[d] Does the use of *Saint* Francis indicate an implicit statement that by canonising him, the church approved his way of life and this is all the writer is asking?

[e] I believe the meaning is accurate here though the translation is a little free as these long Latin sentences

(44-47) do not go well in English where the subject is always the last noun mentioned. Latin is better able to keep track of its subject through numerous sub-clauses.